T0333892

AUTO-INDUSTRIALISM

SAGE SWIFTS

In 1976 SAGE published a series of short 'university papers', which led to the publication of the QASS series (or the 'little green books' as they became known to researchers). Almost 40 years since the release of the first 'little green book', SAGE is delighted to offer a new series of swift, short and topical pieces in the ever-growing digital environment.

SAGE *Swifts* offer authors a new channel for academic research with the freedom to deliver work outside the conventional length of journal articles. The series aims to give authors speedy access to academic audiences through digital first publication, space to explore ideas thoroughly, yet at a length which can be readily digested, and the quality stamp and reassurance of peer-review.

AUTO-INDUSTRIALISM

DIY CAPITALISM AND THE RISE OF THE AUTO-INDUSTRIAL SOCIETY

PETER MURPHY

SAGE SWIFTS

SAGE

Los Angeles | London | New Delhi
Singapore | Washington DC | Melbourne

Los Angeles | London | New Delhi
Singapore | Washington DC | Melbourne

SAGE Publications Ltd
1 Oliver's Yard
55 City Road
London EC1Y 1SP

SAGE Publications Inc.
2455 Teller Road
Thousand Oaks, California 91320

SAGE Publications India Pvt Ltd
B 1/I 1 Mohan Cooperative Industrial Area
Mathura Road
New Delhi 110 044

SAGE Publications Asia-Pacific Pte Ltd
3 Church Street
#10-04 Samsung Hub
Singapore 049483

Editor: Natalie Aguilera
Editorial assistant: Delayna Spencer
Production editor: Vanessa Harwood
Marketing manager: Sally Ransom
Cover design: Jen Crisp
Typeset by: C&M Digitals (P) Ltd, Chennai, India
Printed by CPI Group (UK) Ltd, Croydon, CR0 4YY

Library of Congress Control Number: 2016951859

British Library Cataloguing in Publication data

A catalogue record for this book is available from the British Library

ISBN 978-1-4739-6171-5
eISBN 978-1-4739-9883-4

At SAGE we take sustainability seriously. Most of our products are printed in the UK using FSC papers and boards. When we print overseas we ensure sustainable papers are used as measured by the PREPS grading system. We undertake an annual audit to monitor our sustainability.

Dedicated with much love to Christine Mintrom

CONTENTS

ABOUT THE AUTHOR

Peter Murphy is Adjunct Professor in the School of Humanities and Social Sciences at La Trobe University and Research Fellow in the Cairns Institute at James Cook University. Previously he was Head of the Arts and Creative Media Academic Group, Professor of Arts and Society, and Head of the School of Creative Arts at James Cook University. He has taught at Monash University, The New School for Social Research in New York City, Baylor University in Texas, Victoria University of Wellington, Ateneo de Manila University, and Seoul National University and has been a visiting academic at Ohio State University, Panteion University in Athens, the University of Copenhagen, and Goldsmiths College, University of London. He is the author of *Universities and Innovation Economies* (2015), *The Collective Imagination* (2012) and *Civic Justice* (2001); co-author of *Dialectic of Romanticism: A Critique of Modernism* (2004), *Creativity and the Global Knowledge Economy* (2009), *Global Creation* (2010) and *Imagination* (2010); and co-editor of *Philosophical and Cultural Theories of Music* (2010) and *Aesthetic Capitalism* (2014).

ILLUSTRATION

ACKNOWLEDGEMENTS

While I was writing this book, I benefited from stimulating discussions with Ian Atkinson, Warwick Powell, Craig Browne, Tony Dann, Peter Dansie, Glenn Porter, Thorry Gunnersen, Katja Fleischmann, Ken Friedman, Anders Michelsen, David Salisbury and Chris Hay. Thanks to Chris Rojek for commissioning the book. Some of the material in Chapter 2 is drawn from an article, 'The desktop factory of the new industrial revolution', published in *Quadrant* magazine in October 2014.

INTRODUCTION: THE RISE OF AUTO-INDUSTRIALISM

AUTOMATION AND THE AUTOMATIC SOCIETY

We have entered a period of momentous structural change.[1] For those old enough to remember it, the shift we are experiencing is like that of the 1970s. Then we saw the onset of the post-industrial age. Mass manufacturing industries in the leading economies contracted. Parts of them were exported abroad — to China and elsewhere. The number of well-paid, blue-collar industrial jobs shrank dramatically. Lesser-paying service jobs expanded along with white-collar, professional and para-professional work. The latter was fuelled by an expanding public sector. The government-education-and-health slice of the economy swelled. Theories of human capital and public goods boomed in popularity. This was accompanied in the private sector by the growth of media and communications industries and the information and knowledge economy. Information technology (IT) became pervasive. Computers appeared everywhere. Processes and products were digitized and networked.

The post-industrial world, which we became familiar with, is now itself beginning to disappear. The shift to a markedly different social model — auto-industrialism — is underway. The signs of this are all around us. Go to any big supermarket retailer today and you will see arrays of self-service check-outs. The auto-industrial era is an age of self-service. It is marked by a rising tide of do-it-yourself (DIY), automated and robotic processes. There are continuities with the post-industrial age. The ubiquitous computer remains ubiquitous. However some things are noticeably different. Auto-industrialism does part of what post-industrialism did. But it automates it. Customer-facing retail jobs were standard post-industrial fare. These are now being replaced by automated online purchasing even at bricks-and-mortar locations.

In the United Kingdom, between 2000 and 2015, 750,000 net jobs were lost in manufacturing and 338,000 in wholesale and retail. Two million jobs in that country (60 percent of the current retail workforce) are predicted to disappear from the wholesale and retail sector by 2036.[2] In-store shoppers increasingly prefer to interact with computers that provide information to assist their purchases rather than a sales clerk.[3] Instead of being told by a sales assistant that an item is 'not in stock', machine-mediated retailing can sell customers goods that are not in-store but can be ordered for later pickup or delivery. The phenomenon of 'click-and-collect' goods is on the rise with purchases made online and collected by the customer later from a physical location.[4] The American retailer Macy's is adapting their chain of stores to function as pickup points for online purchasing. Supporting this in the background are computer algorithms that manage the retailer's inventory.[5] Eventually delivery by concierge-style sole contractors and then drones, driverless cars and other robotic means will complete the online purchase system. A pilot is presently being conducted in the United Kingdom of knee-high, shopping cart-sized delivery droids to service the last mile of retail delivery (which currently represents 30 to 40 percent of business delivery costs).[6]

Shops are not disappearing but their functions are changing. They are turning more into collection, experience or try-before-buy destinations than places of assisted sales.[7] The numbers of sales assistants are shrinking.[8] Naturally there is an element of commercial cost-saving in this just as (conversely) there remain customers who prefer the 'personal touch' and expect to deal with a store clerk. Yet it seems that the latter is a smaller cohort than once might have been assumed. Many individuals, it seems, prefer to be left alone when they make purchases.[9] Australians today receive 36 million postal packages annually containing goods they have purchased online. Online retailing in the United Kingdom was 13.5 percent of market share in 2014 and 15.2 percent in 2015.[10] The US figures were 11.6 percent and 12.7 percent, respectively.[11] Each purchase replaces human–human interaction with machine–human interaction. A decade ago, people who booked overseas holiday travel used a travel agent; those numbers today have halved. Self-service, DIY, online ordering-and-paying has visibly reduced the industry. Large numbers of people have decided that the time cost of doing-it-yourself outweighs the service value of a white-collar, or rather T-shirted, industry operator doing it for you. Even in the realm of high culture, similar kinds of changes are occurring. Online art galleries are becoming increasingly important. They are in part displacing physical galleries. André Malraux's 'museum without walls' is being realized. Human–machine interaction provides individuals with ready access to artworks whenever and from wherever.

Machine automation is an expression of a deeper social shift. The growth of participation in and enjoyment of human–machine interaction over the historic term indicates increasing levels of comfort with an automated society. This is a distinctive kind of modern society. It is one that is dominated by the impersonal patterns of markets, industries, cities and publics.[12] In an automated society, economic and social cycles, ratios, fractals and proportions play a decisive role in long-term social development. They play a more decisive part than do directives, regulations, procedures, policies or rules. The tendency to automate social functioning is characteristic of high-functioning modern societies and economies. These have, to a notable extent, an impersonal, autonomously operating, self-regulating nature. They are animated by business, technology, political and urban cycles, phases and relations that have a quasi-life of their own. The price-to-earnings ratio, the debt-to-GDP ratio, the ideal or 'golden' ratio, the Fibonacci number series, the power law of city size, the Pareto (80–20) principle of cause-and-effect and scaling laws (like the quantity theory of money) provide constants in dynamic growth-orientated societies. These constants are not legislated; they are not tools for social engineering. They are not instruments designed for state intervention. Rather they provide durable form in fluid social environments. These environments change rapidly and yet their underlying principles are remarkably stable over time.

Social laws in a world of freedom, surely not?[13] Yet the paradox is that societal self-regulation and machine automation, far from being hostile to human freedom, are conducive to high levels of personal autonomy and individual freedom.[14] The impersonal in this case strengthens the personal. At the level of industrial automation, impersonal interaction with machines allows individuals to more readily do things for themselves and reduces the pressures that accompany everyday functional and official relationships. Assuming it works well, human–machine interaction reduces the pressure of sales talk. It alleviates the strain of dealing with petty officials and counter clerks. It removes the pain of listening to the spurious chatter of real estate agents. It obviates the ill-informed advice of the town council's trainee planning assistant. In short, it reduces the tiny coercions of everyday public life.

Machines do not suit everyone. Some people prefer dealing with other people than dealing with machines. They resolutely resist the use of appliances and devices. Yet the popularity of automated teller machines (ATMs) for bank cash withdrawals suggests that technophobic attitudes to new generations of machines shrink over time. The first ATM was installed in 1969; there are now three million of these machines worldwide. Such is the nature of industrialism that even machines are replaced by machines. Today electronic funds transfer at point of sale is gradually reducing the use of ATMs. The human condition is such that human beings are double-coded. They see themselves through their relationship with other human beings. They place great value on inter-subjective relationships. At the same time, human beings create their own artificial environment. This is a 'second nature', consisting of made objects and artifices.[15] It is composed of material items, buildings, tools and machines. Human beings surround themselves with objects. They make, buy, use, love and appreciate objects. They inhabit a world of objects. This world is a second nature, an artificial nature that complements the first nature of plants and animals.

Human beings have a creative impulse. They like to give form and shape to things. They husband animals; garden plants and flowers; hammer wood; bolt steel; arrange pixels; code bits and bytes. This shaping or forming impulse is closely connected to the human identification with the symmetries, boundaries, cycles, waves and proportions of nature. In making beautiful things that are also useful, nature is recreated in a second nature, the object world of humankind. Cities, buildings, tools, machines and personal artefacts all belong to this object world. This explains the great affection individuals show towards trains, planes and cars, or their computers and mobile phones. This does not detract from the pleasure they have in interacting with other human beings. The object-world and the subject-world are not mutually exclusive. So auto-industrialism is not a threat to human relationships any more than the automobile was. This does not stop technophobic literary forms from imagining otherwise though. A civilization that loves its machines also loves to depict those machines rising up and taking over. But aside from cultural projections of fears and anxieties, auto-industrialism does not imply human alienation. Rather it does what all automation does: it eliminates routine work, both manual and intellectual. As interactions with machines increase, individuals still have intense personal interactions with others: with family, friends and acquaintances.[16] But they opt out of other more procedural, instrumental and mundane interactions with their fellow human beings. In place of those prosaic exchanges, they instead opt for human–machine transactions because of their convenience and lack of pressure.

The volume of human–machine interactions is rising. Self-organizing machines are becoming increasingly common in everyday life. There are many examples of these: house vacuuming robots (Roomba), companion bots (Jibo), bartending bots (Monsieur), the multilingual retail bot (OSHbot) along with algorithm-driven market trading, automated intelligent searching of legal and medical records, autonomous weapons systems (Super Aegis), facial recognition surveillance software, market and opinion survey robocalls, voice recognition validation software, robotic healthcare assistants (Baymax) and self-driving vehicles. American's Defence Advanced Research Projects Agency was crucial in the development of the Internet. Now it is developing the robotic battlefield. Japan today plans to take on China industrially with a massive program of robot factories. Foxconn, the giant Taiwan-based iPhone manufacturer, projects its own program of automation. Mainland China meanwhile is beginning a vigorous transition from factory labour to robots.[17]

How many commercial truck drivers or taxi drivers or fork-lift drivers will there be in 30 years' time? Likely, not many. The mining company Rio Tinto already operates autonomous haulage vehicles, drillers, ore dumpers, stackers and reclaimers in its mines. Farm robots will weed, prune, monitor produce, check on herds and harvest crops. The globalization era saw the export of traditional manufacturing jobs from developed to developing countries. Skilled jobs were replaced with service jobs. Now service jobs are being automated. Lowe's, the US hardware retailer, is trialling humanoid robot shop assistants. Japan plans robot nursing home assistants to cope with its aged population. Health assistants are one of the prime projected employment growth areas in the next 20 years. But what if these jobs are gradually replaced by machines? There are lots of long-term scenarios for wealth creation but few for job creation. Keeping in mind that jobs are a subset of occupations, it may turn out in the future that job creation is gradually overtaken by occupation creation in the self-employed sector.[18]

Peopleless robot factories and driverless vehicles will transform labour markets. Many existing jobs will be eliminated. This applies not only to blue-collar work but also to pink-collar, white-collar, service and professional work. Low-level medical diagnoses, preparation of tax returns, paralegal document searches and university essay marking in the foreseeable future will be automated. The same is happening already to the work of book-keepers, marketers and meter readers. Self-service is taking over airline check-in and supermarket check-outs. Any formula task can be automated. A lot of professional operations, as we are discovering, are just that: formulas. Some professional disciplines are finding that they cannot match the power of big data processing. Pattern recognition software for instance will replace much of radiology diagnostics.

These are new developments but in a way also very old ones. The mix of computing, digital sensing and robotic handling on a mass scale is new. Yet the underlying driver of this, automation, is a fixture of industrial societies. It is a function as much of the essential continuity as it is of the perpetual change of industrial societies. It represents the essence or nature of industrialism. Automation is a fixity amidst technological mutability; a variable invariant. Through more intense and less intense periods, it substitutes machines for hand, back and brain power. Today the spread of new generations of self-organizing machines is starting to have a visible impact on labour markets. This impact is being felt not just in one or two job market segments but rather across the full spectrum of service, blue-collar, white-collar, pink-collar, professional and para-professional work. The graduate employment market accordingly is shrinking.[19] The mass demand for individuals with undergraduate degrees is declining relative to the demand for high school graduates and university postgraduates. The structure of the labour market is being reshaped. This is a consequence of long-term technology and employment trends. These trends reflect the shift from post-industrialization to auto-industrialization.

THE END OF POST-INDUSTRIALISM

Post-industrialization represented a tectonic change in the structure of employment. In the 1970s, Australia manufactured 500,000 cars annually and employed 90,000 workers in the auto industry. As of 2017 it will produce zero cars. In the 1970s and 1980s across the OECD, manufacturing industries declined. Factories were shuttered or relocated aboard. Middle-income blue-collar work shrank. The public policy question then arose: what would replace these jobs? The answer was white-collar 'knowledge' work. Universities and colleges, it was thought, would educate the 'knowledge' workers of the future. What was the effect of that? Today a quarter or more of graduates never work in a job that requires a degree. As the size of the university and college sector grew so did the number of graduates working as taxi drivers.[20] Human capital economics assumed that education determines economic outcomes. If anything, the reverse is the case. As enrolment numbers at universities expanded, the relative size of median graduate salaries shrank.[21] Since 1990, the relative number of middle-income salaried jobs has shrunk as well.

After 1970, in the leading industrial nations the scale of manufacturing decreased. The contraction of manufacturing was driven by industry economics. Cheap labour abroad beckoned. Alternatively when factories stayed put, machines replaced labour. Work was automated. This reflected the logic of industrial society which is to substitute machines for routine labour. Post-industrialization coincided with a political and cultural shift in major states. Social expectations were transformed by big government liberalism. In the post-industrial era, the focus of political attention shifted from production to distribution. The welfare state burgeoned. Crony capitalism multiplied. Grants and allocations captured the social imagination. Government debt and deficits increased. This debt was illusory money. It was easy to obtain but difficult to pay off.

The long-term consequences of post-industrialization were in many respects sullen. In advanced economies, the great wealth creation phase of the 1950s and 1960s stopped. Long-term real income and GDP growth flattened. Pundits promised that the workforce would become populated with glamorous highly educated symbol-users. University enrolments exploded. The class of public sector professionals and administrators swelled. The focus of post-industrialism was document production and rule generation. Fifteen percent of the GDP of advanced economies today is consumed by regulation. Even then not everyone can be a document fabricator or rule processor. The alternative usually is a service job. Today graduates wait tables and drive taxis. Increasing numbers of people opt out of work altogether into government disability payment schemes.[22] In the post-industrial era the moral crux of modern life, the work ethic, came under mounting strain.

Today, for the first time in 40 years, there are tentative signs of a reaction against this. Post-industrialism has run its course. Twentieth-century Keynesian economics supposed that employment was a function of economic demand and that such demand could be stimulated by government spending.[23] Time and again that has proved not to be the case. This is because economies are foremost a function of supply and production rather than demand and distribution. If economies fail to supply appealing goods, they falter. The popular music industry boomed in the 1960s and 1970s when it produced interesting artefacts. It is desultory today by comparison because it no longer does that. At times it blames the Internet for its woes. But the real cause of its decline is that it is one among many industries in the post-industrial period that lost its capacity to produce exciting or attractive goods.

Over the long run the wealth-creating power of modern industrial capitalism has been remarkable. What has driven it has been the ability to create ingenious new products of lasting value, interest and utility. Equally remarkable have been the canny ways devised for producing these products. The first industrial revolution gave us the putting-out system (cottage industry). The factory system followed. After that we had the production line, the firm and the modern organization. The least effective of all of these was 'the organization'. It dominated the post-industrial information age. This was the era of electronic documents and office software. While its advocates periodically promised the coming of the lean corporation, the principal legacy of IT in the post-industrial period was the relentless expansion of private and public bureaucracies. These produced mountains of unproductive intangibles — reports, audits, assessments, reviews and regulatory frameworks. This documentary megalith was reflected in declining productivity and shrinking real wealth creation across the era.[24]

From 1970 to 1990 the post-industrial script outwardly looked credible. The classic middle tier of industrial skilled work shrivelled but low-income service work, middle-income administrative and sales work and high-income high-tier professional work grew. Yet under the surface, another story began to take shape. This centred on the phenomenon of 'job polarization'.[25] This development began to crystallize in 1990.[26] It was first defined analytically in 2003.[27] Job polarization means the shrinking of middle-tier, middle-income work relative to low-income service work and high-income, high-end professional work. This is a function of technology. Both manual and office work are affected. Computerization today is eliminating routine administrative, service and retail work at an accelerating pace. Robots are replacing machine operators, assembly and production workers, miners and wharf labour. The mid-tier of occupations is contracting. At the same time, demand for low-skill service work has grown. A particular kind of service work (in security, cleaning, care and hospitality) requires manual dexterity. Such work (so far) has been resistant to automation. Demand for it has grown along with the demand for high-skill professional abstract labour that involves significant elements of interpretation, invention, judgement or creativity. The labour market in advanced economies is starting to look like an hour-glass, with growth at the top and the bottom and shrinkage in the middle.

As a result of job polarization, the second half of the post-industrial era (the period between 1990 and 2010) started to generate an employment structure that was the opposite of what post-industrialization was meant to achieve. The effects of this incipient reversal have become clearer over time. Graduate employment in low-skill service occupations has grown. The premium received by young adults getting degrees (today 30 percent or more of them) has shrunk. In the 1950s, college graduates in the United States earned 2.3 times that of high school graduates. Now they earn 2.5 times a person with 8 years only of education. In many advanced economies, median income has flattened while the career income of the 10 percent of the young adult population who today undertake some kind of postgraduate degree has increased.[28] The percentage of the population in 2005 getting PhDs was about the same percentage of the population getting undergraduate degrees in 1955. Large numbers of young adults now go to university. However, the principal beneficiary of contemporary higher education is the small postgraduate class whose labour is abstract. Demand, as expressed in income, continues to grow in the case of the relatively small 10 percent of the workforce whose labour leans heavily on calculation, interpretation, judgement, problem solving, reflexivity, coordination, ingenuity, resourcefulness, imagination, originality, innovation and creativity. In the near run, over the next decade demand is projected to be especially high for calculation-based expertise in business and financial operations, mathematics and computing. In contrast, the demand for qualified mid-tier salaried employees doing tasks that are well-defined, organized into clear analytical steps and firmly demarcated from other tasks — in short that are recurring, routine and methodical — is shrinking. Machines are replacing people in these roles.

Where post-industrialism eviscerated manufacturing work in advanced economies, auto-industrial technologies are now eliminating routine work.[29] This includes routine manual, office, sales, service, para-professional and low-end professional work.[30] As this technology wave further unfolds over the next 10 and 20 years, much existing routine mid-tier pink-collar, white-collar and ancillary professional work will disappear. This has multiple implications. The need for mass higher education is shrinking. The world of 'the office' and the 'sales department' staffed by middle-income workers with generic university degrees, doing defined repetitive tasks, is collapsing.[31] Computerization and automation are replacing these kinds of employees.[32] Thirty to forty percent of current occupations will be significantly affected by computerization and automation in the next 10 years. In effect, a net 15 to 20 percent of current jobs will disappear. The era of large-scale routine knowledge work is powering down. This change is occurring persistently on a large scale and over the long term. As manufacturing work in the 1970s was automated and offshored, routine office, sales and para-professional work is similarly being automated or offshored.

By 2045 few mid-tier 'knowledge jobs' will be left. Whether for society this means structural unemployment or underemployment or else different kinds of occupation at this point in time is unclear. Mid-tier wage-and-salary work in accommodation, food, transport, real estate, retail sales, wholesale, manufacturing and mining will be reduced by automation. The prospect of alternate wage-and-salary employment in new labour-intensive industries appears slim though demand for certain kinds of dexterous manual occupations is growing not declining. Auto-industrial technologies will spawn distinctive occupations. Yet it is unlikely that these will generate the multiples of the kinds of mid-tier wage-and-salary jobs that early- and mid-twentieth-century manufacturing industry did in the major economies of the time. The foreseeable effect of auto-industrialization will be the further reduction of mid-tier wage-and-salary employment.

Does this then mean high rates of unemployment? This is unlikely to be the case in societies with aging and shrinking populations that are prepared to restrict the flow of migrants into their workforce. In such cases, automation and robotics will simply replace persons retiring and exiting the workforce. Furthermore automation will not affect all occupations. Demand for manually dextrous service work that robots (yet) cannot do and for high-end abstract professional labour foreseeably will be sustained and conceivably will even expand. Current American 10-year projections of labour demand indicate near-term high growth in financial management, health, construction and personal services. The latter three include considerable demand for persons with high school-only qualifications.

Also notable is a long-term trend for individuals in major economies to generate income from capital rather than labour. Capital work has partially replaced wage-and-salary work. The self-employed sector including sole traders and partnerships has been growing over the long run. This shift is subtly reshaping the nature of work and occupations. The trend for 'income from capital' to grow relative to 'income from wage labour' began in the 1950s. It accelerated in the 1970s. It appears that it will persist, deepen and intensify in the foreseeable future.[33] This means that if there is a future expansion of mid-tier occupations these will most likely be sourced from the self-employed workforce. Demand for entrepreneurial nous is replacing demand for labour skills. Salaried work is declining and capital work is increasing.

An analogous shift is reflected in the behaviour of traditional firms and their hiring practices. Around 2010 a new company hiring trend began to crystallize.[34] This is a preference for employees with a mix of digital know-how, agility, creativity, entrepreneurship, problem solving and negotiating ability.[35] If we add to that list additional traits — like dexterity, adroitness, nimbleness, and a capacity to decipher, elucidate, unravel and decode — a picture starts to emerge of the nature of the auto-industrial era employee.[36] If a short-hand term is needed to sum up auto-industrial work, it would be problem solving. It does not matter whether we are talking about manual, office or professional work, problem solving stands in contrast to the processing fixation of post-industrial work. Post-industrialism was built on a workforce engaged in routine detailed step-by-step process and procedure. This type of work followed well-defined pathways. If in the future machines increasingly do this kind of path-dependent work then what remains is nimble work. In the case of nimble work, tasks are not well defined, predictable or well rehearsed. This is irrespective of whether the task is physical, mental or both. Nimble work requires the ability to change orientation swiftly and initiate unpredicted or unusual sequences of actions. Metaphors of intellectual and physical swinging, spiralling, flipping, gyrating, rotating, turning and self-starting apply to this kind of work.

Self-starting, problem-solving and adroit behaviours have increasing value in the auto-industrial age. Self-management in place of other-directed decision making is at a premium. But not all of contemporary culture is in sync with this — far from it. Take the case of higher education. In 2015, 20 percent of UK university students surveyed said that they wanted to work for a large company and 34 percent for a medium-sized company. Only 6 percent of British students said they wanted to run their own business and only 10 percent wished to work for a start-up company.[37] Yet the underlying logic of the auto-industrial age favours small start-up companies, partnerships and sole proprietorships.[38] Most net new employment today is generated by small businesses that are less than 5 years old with less than 250 staff and especially those with less than 50 staff.[39] Auto-industrialism is in step with the larger historical trend for 'income from capital' to grow relative to 'income from wages and salaries'.[40]

While auto-industrialism favours self-starters, post-industrial culture does not.[41] This means that inherited social expectations are now at odds with contemporary social trends. Received expectations have been shaped by five decades of post-industrialization. The larger part of the twentieth century was dominated philosophically by state socialism. Government employment in major economies grew significantly. After 1970, a shift occurred. This was the era of post-industrial neo-socialism and social liberalism. The government sector continued to grow but this was matched and exceeded by the growth of the broader taxpayer-subsidized education and health sectors. Governmental, education and health lobbies all relied on something called 'knowledge' as their legitimation. These voluble interest groups each claimed they produced public goods or public benefits that embodied 'expertise', 'intelligence', 'know-how' and 'information'. The reality though was somewhat different. What taxpayers paid for on an ever-escalating scale was process and administration. Ever larger portions of perpetually mounting education and health spending was not for education or health functions in the literal sense but rather for the bureaucratic processes and procedures that surrounded them. Intelligence was a euphemism for officialdom. The documentation of process was knowledge. Since the late nineteenth century, government service was legitimated even sanctified by claims to special knowledge or expertise. Such legitimations were intended to incite awe and mystery. The claim of government administrators to special knowledge was underwritten in the nineteenth century by civil service examinations. In the twentieth century, the university degree replaced the legitimating function of the examination. As government grew, followed by public sector education and health, administration grew. Armed with university qualifications battalions of administrators, officers, supervisors, managers, directors and executives populated the swelling ranks of education, health and government systems. They endowed these institutions with an aura of indispensable self-importance.

Auto-industrialization represents the end of the post-industrial era. The age of the government, health and education juggernaut is over. This is not for ideological or political reasons. In the 1980s, there was a period when the post-industrial expansion of the public sector and public subsidies was questioned, mainly in the Anglosphere. But this affected only the rate of expansion of the public sector. By the late 1990s and 2000s, the expansion was redoubled. Taxpayer-funded or -subsidized jobs for teachers, nurses and care workers boomed (the latter pushed along by aging populations).[42] Many expect this trend to continue in the future on the grounds that these are high-touch occupations immune from automation.[43] This assumption though is questionable. Digitization offers serious prospects for the semi-automation online of higher education.[44] The 'do-it-yourself university' utilizing the vast store of open source content accessible on computers and phones has overtaken the historic function of adult education. There are a variety of ways of thinking about this. One is self-education. Autodidactic models are already common in the IT industry. We will likely see the spread of self-education to other sectors. One of the keys to this is competency-based degree-granting. This requires reputable examining bodies to offer serious testing of competency leading to a degree but without all the baggage of classes, tuition costs, campuses and car parks.[45]

A person who is disciplined and motivated does not necessarily require any more than the unlimited resources of the Internet to learn and a rigorous independent examining body in order to acquire a degree that has vocational power and credible standing. In truth, many of the best minds are self-taught whether they attend classes or not.[46] For those who are less autodidactic in spirit, the degree-granting 'platform university' (with automated administration, micro-campuses, online delivery and third-place meet-ups in disperse locations) is another conceivable option on the horizon.[47] Robotics will deliver much in the way of rote learning technology in the same way in the 1970s the digital calculator replaced the manual slide rule. The patience of the robot in coping with the slow learner far exceeds that of any human being. Similarly in care and nursing, the scope for robotic care, diagnostic aids and self-monitoring is large. In occupations like teaching, nursing and care, it is often underestimated how much of the work is routine, repetitive and how much of it requires the kind of infinite patience that human beings lack.

Computers and robots are well suited to doing repetitive tasks. Consequently machines graced with various kinds of artificial intelligence (AI) have no better or more plausible application than in government. The scope that exists for shrinking government by automating it is enormous. Yet the nature of the state is such that it is always disposed to increase the size of officialdom rather than decrease it. This implies that the automation of government administration will be resisted. 'Jobs' will be the cry; 'you are replacing good jobs with machines'. Indeed so, for that is the nature of industrial societies. The question is whenever jobs in a society are lost whether different kinds of occupations will arise to replace what has gone.

There are varying scenarios concerning this. One, the optimistic scenario, says that overall technological change creates more jobs than it destroys.[48] That does not obviate the depth of change, though. In industrial societies even over relatively modest historical intervals, the elimination of jobs is quite remarkable. In 1870, 50 percent of jobs in the United States were in agriculture; by 1900, that figure had fallen to 38 percent. Today the figure is 2 percent. Robotics will soon transform the remaining areas in agriculture where work is still performed by hand. Automation and mechanization are not new phenomena. They are part of the nature of industrialism. In an industrial society machines regularly replace repetitive work of all kinds — and have done so since the eighteenth century when industrial machines first appeared. Human–machine interaction is an essential part of living in an industrial society, whether the machine is a train, an automobile, an airplane, a computer or a robot.

A second, more sceptical scenario suggests that the first scenario was true until the post-industrial era but since then a shift has occurred. Either fewer jobs or fewer mid-tier jobs have been created; unemployment is disguised by the proliferation of persons on disability benefits or the decrease in labour market participation. Major employers in new industries like IT employ far fewer people than large employers did in the era of classic mass manufacturing. In response to this a third, more optimistic scenario says that the second scenario is true but is offset by self-employment that is growing relative to salaried employment. The third scenario takes issue with technological pessimism and with knowledge economy boosters alike. The tendency of technology change to stimulate basic fears has been long evident. Dark science fiction fantasies seem to follow the advance of computerization and robotics. Consequently, we will have more stories about cyborgs that have feelings, go on rampages, cause chaos, feign being human, kill us, meld with human beings, self-replicate, become conscious and eventually replace human beings.

In a more prosaic vein, we will also have overexcited depictions of future mass joblessness. These will try and induce us to adopt guaranteed minimum income schemes.[49] These schemes are designed to ensure that everyone has a basic income whether they work or not.[50] They are specious. The modern welfare state already has endless schemes that guarantee income; all of these programs ironically though are dependent on the continued growth of wealth itself, in turn, dependent on technological development. Portrayals of mass technological unemployment, like the rise of Skynet, the conscious AI in the *Terminator* movie, tap human anxieties in industrial societies. This does not make them anything more than fictions.

The future looks rather more enticing than the pessimists suggest. Unconsciously they wish for a kind of neo-feudal welfare state. The state they envisage is populated by workless masses who live on minimum incomes. The machines have taken all the jobs. Income is transferred by a benevolent state elite from the technologically crafty corporate elite. Whether this is depicted in dystopian or utopian terms, or both, the instinct is neo-patrimonial. The morbid vision of mass technological unemployment is a hook upon which to raise up, yet again, another client-patron model of society.[51] This vision seems ineradicable, whether it is the ancient Roman dole, medieval feudalism, modern socialism, post-modern rent seeking or auto-industrial minimum income schemes. That said, even if (as probable) mass technological unemployment does not eventuate, far-reaching changes in the character and type of employment are on the cards. Tomorrow will not be business-as-usual. There are major structural social changes afoot. These involve the reshaping of occupational structures, the nature of work, the relation between capital and labour and the relation between human beings and machines. This social reshaping will be deep-going, confronting and painful. It will challenge many cherished expectations. It will demolish many truisms about work and wealth. It will upset many people. Welcome to the auto-industrial age.

NOTES

1. Some like Schwab (2016) have called it a fourth industrial revolution.
2. Chan (2016).
3. Deloitte (2014: 27).
4. Forty percent of London Internet sales are 'click and collect'. Though only a small portion of overall sales, they are increasing at 30–40 percent a year compared with the less than 3 percent growth in total retail sales. Deloitte (2014: 27).
5. Skorupa (2013); Joe (2013).
6. Telegraph Reporters (2016).
7. Models such as 'research online buy offline' (robo) and 'click and collect' are gradually replacing the conventional store sales formula.
8. The United Kingdom between 2001 and 2014 lost 72,000 retail cashier and check-out jobs and 69,000 wholesale and retail shopkeepers and proprietors (Deloitte, 2015a: 7).
9. Aided by online comparisons with other products and retailers as well as online reviews of products by other shoppers.

10. Centre for Retail Research (2015).
11. The online retail market share in Europe and Australia is in the 7–10 percent range.
12. Murphy, 2015b.
13. On the history of the idea of social laws, see Brown (1984).
14. As with all social shifts, there are contrary forces at work. Online anonymity is conducive to social distance and independence. At times though, it also elicits furious umbrage, foot-stamping and shouting designed to put pressure on others.
15. Murphy and Roberts (2004: 83–6) and Murphy (2014b).
16. This does not guarantee that in every instance persons will always prefer other people over machines. Disengaging from others is as old as the human species itself.
17. 'More than 100 industrial robots have been installed at a zero-labor factory that is being built in Dongguan, a major manufacturing base in Guangdong province. The construction of the factory, the first of its kind in the province, marks an important step for the "robot assembly line" strategy that is being followed by the province as it tackles a severe labor shortage. Chen Qixing, chairman of the board of Guangdong Everwin Precision Technology, said 1,000 robots will be used in the first phase of the production facility. "The use of industrial robots will help the company to reduce the number of front-line workers by at least 90 percent," Chen said. "When all the 1,000 industrial robots are put into operation in the coming months, we will only need to recruit fewer than 200 software technicians and management personnel"' (Zheng, 2015).
18. As James Bennett and Michael Lotus (2013: 186) observe: 'the entire concept of a "job" is going away. At the time of the Founding, most Americans did not have jobs. There is no reason to think most Americans in the future will have jobs, primarily working at the direction of others employing capital owned by others. Americans are not yet remotely prepared for this shift, either institutionally, or psychologically.'
19. In an interview in 2014, Catherine Livingstone, the President of the Business Council of Australia, said that Australian universities were enrolling too many domestic students. Ian Young, Vice Chancellor of the Australian National University, added that Australia's major research universities would enrol fewer students in the future if given the chance (Gilmore and Knott, 2014).
20. Murphy (2015a: 170).
21. Murphy (2015a: 192–201).
22. Since 1990, the share of the American working-age population that receives disability benefits has doubled, increasing from 1 in 40 persons to 1 in 20 (Boccia, 2015). An aging population and an older retirement age explains a small portion of this shift. More significant still is the combination of broader definitions of disability, looser application of entitlement criteria and a growing social readiness to see the long-term receipt of disability benefits as an alternative to paid work. As American industries have got safer, the portion of the population receiving disability benefits has grown.
23. Spending spurred the rise of the grant-request industry (lobbies and pressure groups) and grant-funded industries. Both distorted sound economic behaviour.

24. Gordon (2016) characterizes this as a 'slow growth period since 1975' (averaging 1.2 percent p.a.); technologically, he avers, 'we have achieved relatively slow progress since 1970' notwithstanding the spread of computers. 'The period 1870 to 1970 was a special century when it comes to technology-driven productivity increases (averaging 2 percent p.a.). The century was unique in human history and unrepeatable because the achievements of the era could only happen once. The combination of electricity, the internal combustion engine, water utilities, and the conquest of infant mortality made this an exceptional hundred years, the like of which we will not see again. In contrast, computing and the Internet are not nearly as significant although productivity did accelerate briefly in the dot.com decade between 1995 and 2005 as a consequence of information technology.' The counterargument to this Murphy (2015a) agrees that a slowdown in innovation and growth occurred after 1970 but that this was the result of post-industrialization which was unable to deliver significant productivity increases in service industries including office industries. Rather than becoming more efficient, office work became relatively more inefficient as organizations became increasingly bureaucratized.

25. Autor and Dorn (2013) and Autor, Katz and Kearney (2006).

26. More sceptically, Schmitt, Shierholz and Mishel (2013) argue that labour market job polarization has been going on since the 1950s. Their thesis is that mid-skill occupational employment has declined and high-skill occupational employment has increased in every decade since the 1950s while demand for high-wage occupations fell in the 2000s.

27. Goos and Manning (2003) and Autor, Levy and Murnane (2003).

28. Murphy (2015a: 197–8).

29. Frey and Osborne (2013, 2015).

30. Autor, Katz and Kearney (2006) and Autor and Dorn (2013).

31. In the United Kingdom, between 2001 and 2014, 58,000 business sales executive jobs were lost along with 204,000 personal assistants and secretaries and 108,000 typists and keyboard occupations (Deloitte, 2015a: 7).

32. Frey and Osborne's research for Deloitte (2014) on the UK workforce in the next 10–20 years projects a large decline in white-collar office, retail and service jobs (figure 2). In the period 2001–13 in London, the number of library assistants, sales occupations, record assistants, travel agents, counter staff, PAs and secretaries and bookkeepers declined sharply (figure 4).

33. One tacit advantage of this accrues to countries with aging populations. As people age they exit the workforce, no longer earning income from wages and salaries, but if they have capital assets (stock portfolios, rental properties, etc.) they will continue to generate income. This corrects for the problem that Robert Gordon (2016) points to that, namely that with an increasing percentage of the population out of the active workforce in aging societies, future labour productivity gains (measured as increased output per employee per hour) have to be spread among a greater number of people (via wages and transfer payments) as labour retires. However, productivity is not only

the productivity of labour but of all the factors of production. The return on capital investment is also a means of spreading the benefits of productivity increases. In contemporary aging societies, if the same output can be produced with less labour, the effect will be increased productivity whose benefits are expressed not only in real wages or tax-derived transfer payments but also in the return on capital investments.

34. Kern, 2010.

35. Deloitte (2014, figure 12).

36. Not as well understood is the correlated need of management to be less risk-averse, less rule-driven and less micro-managing.

37. Barea and Vasudeva (2015).

38. 14.7 percent of the UK workforce is sole proprietors; in Australia, it is 9 percent. Eleven percent of the US workforce is sole proprietors, working more than 15 hours a week and many working more than 35 hours a week; another 7 percent work less than 15 hours a week (Johnson, 2013; MBO Partners, 2014; Committee for Economic Development of Australia, 2015: 180). This is a contented workforce. Fifteen percent of US sole proprietors who work more than 15 hours a week earn an income of $100,000 or more a year (MBO Partners, 2014: 4, 5, 8, 12).

39. Stangler (2010, figures 3–5). This phenomenon is echoed by the UK IoD99 small business enterprise culture peer network. Since 1990, in the United States big business eliminated four million jobs and small businesses have added eight million new jobs. Data source: US Small Business Administration.

40. This trend is reflected in the rise in the numbers and income of sole proprietors. In the United States in 1995, there were 16,423,000 sole proprietor tax returns. In 2012, the number was 23,426,000, an increase of 42 percent in 18 years. Over the same period, the population of the United States increased by 22 percent only. The total business receipts of sole traders grew from $807 billion to $1,301 billion, outpacing inflation by 7 percent. Data source: Internal Revenue Service sole proprietorship returns 1996 and 2012.

41. It also favours persons with broad, flexible, agile talents. Post-industrialism was the age of qualifications. Auto-industrialism is the era of DIY multi-skilling. Transdisciplinary abilities accordingly are much sought-after. From 1970 to 2000, demand for IT specialists boomed. Then the IT bubble burst. Today, where the professional market flourishes is not in traditional IT roles but in hybrid IT-business-organizational roles (Glover, 2011; Miller, 2011). Qualifications are anchored in disciplines; the DIY capability to synthesize elements of business, science, technology and the arts is closer to the inward spirit of auto-industrialism. The DIY talent is related to creative ability. Both take what is set apart and fuse it together. See, e.g., Dyer, Gregersen and Christensen (2011: 41–64).

42. In the United Kingdom, jobs for teaching assistants, secondary, primary and nursery and other educational professionals grew by 235,000, 131,000, 110,000 and 113,000 respectively; jobs for nurses grew by 186,000; and jobs for care workers and home carers grew by 271,000 (Deloitte, 2015: 7).

43. This assumption is made by Frey and Osborne (2013, 2015), whose influential analytic work provides the best current projections of which occupations will be least and most affected by automation. They assume that teaching, nursing and care occupations will be largely immune from automation.

44. Kamenetz (2010); Reynolds (2014); Murphy (2016).

45. Championed by Wisconsin governor Scott Walker, the University of Wisconsin began offering competency-based bachelor's degrees in 2013 (Porter, 2013), while Dennis (2014) notes that the multi-state Western Governors University 'has awarded college degrees based on assessments of learning since 1997'. These and other recent initiatives at Purdue University and University of Michigan seem largely motivated by the interest in having students with some existing traditional degree credit complete their degrees rather than a beginning-to-end system of DIY education. Nonetheless, they provide the basis for fully autonomous higher education.

46. Those who did not go to a university or college include Richard Branson, Michael Dell, James Cameron, Benjamin Franklin and Abigail Adams. http://selfmadescholar.com/

47. Murphy (2016).

48. Stewart, Debapratim and Cole (2015).

49. An N-gram search shows that the concept of a guaranteed minimum income had a brief spectacular career between 1962 and 1972 and then just as suddenly fell out of favour. The reason for its 1960s' popularity was that it promised an income separate from employment in an era of escalating automation.

50. Ford (2015). Sachs (2015) similarly presses for the redistribution of income in order for us to live happily with robots. Sachs, Benzell and LaGarda (2015) argue that the increase in robotic productivity will lower wages in the long run and that this 'immiserization' of labour can only be overcome through the 'redistributive policies of the state'. Megan McCardle (2013) sets out four reasons why a guaranteed minimum income will not work: (1) Take all the welfare benefits in the United States and distribute them to all 235 million adults: that amounts to $3,000 per adult per year. Providing a viable minimum income for (say) a quarter of all adults would amount to an infeasible doubling (at least) of the welfare bill. (2) A guaranteed income would reduce the reciprocity at the heart of a functioning society by creating an entitlement without the corresponding duty to contribute. (3) A minimum income state would be a magnet for illegal immigrants seeking to receive benefits without making contributions. (4) Long-term minimum income recipients would experience difficulty re-entering the job market.

51. On the historic conflict between the patrimonial model of society and the countervailing model of proportionality, see Murphy (2001).

I

WORK

THE ROBOTS ARE COMING

A lot of the technology that the auto-industrial society uses is familiar to us. This is typical of technological change. It begins slowly. It tends to have a long gestation period before being widely applied. The idea of automation is an old one. In classical Greek antiquity, Aristotle speculated about machines that moved by themselves. He imagined self-moving looms and lyres. He thought that if such machines were to exist then neither servants nor slaves would be necessary. Little under the sun is new. There were designs for automata in the ancient Hellenistic period. Leonardo da Vinci sketched an idea for a robot knight. Nicolas-Joseph Cugnot's first approximation of the automobile — a steam-powered tricycle — appeared in 1769. Karl Benz's similarly tricyclical Motorwagen was patented in 1886. Ransom Olds began factory production of automobiles in 1902 in Lansing Michigan. The same kind of slow-burning development is true for robotics as well. The Czech playwright Karel Čapek coined the term 'robot' in 1920.[1] Norbert Wiener formulated the theoretical principles of robotics in 1948. The first factory robot, the Unimate, was installed in a Trenton New Jersey plant in 1961.

Since the rise of the automobile, and then the personal computer, human–machine interactions have become pervasive. This reflects the fact that human beings on the whole are comfortable with machines — not just at work but also at home. People get endeared to their cars. They populate their houses with washing machines and dish washers. Computing devices become extensions of themselves — indispensable, convenient, personalized, necessary and time-saving. After two decades of personal computing, things that once would have been unthinkable are now very conceivable. In the future much aged care assistance will gradually be turned over to robots of one kind or another.

The novelty of this will quickly disappear and care-bots will seem no more unusual in a person's life than an automobile. In many cases they will provide auto-mobility. They will also reduce the incidence of abuse and cruelty in nursing homes where repetitive daily feeding and cleaning tasks breed anger and hostility in support staff. That robotic machines are unfeeling, like personal computers, is a plus not a minus. Not all human feelings are good. Nor are all human interactions beneficial. Take the case of autistic children. Two of the impediments to autistic children learning are their short attention spans and the fact that human facial expressions overstimulate them. This makes teaching them in a regular way difficult. An instructor or parent has to have endless patience in repeating the same exercise. Dispensing with facial expressions is even more difficult. But this is not so for robot instructors. They run the same routines endlessly; and they do not have to have faces, just voices.

The history of technology is one of long slow development punctuated by dramatic upswings. Successful technologies evolve slowly and then take off. Currently we seem to be in a take-off period. The vacuum cleaner robot, Roomba, illustrates the point. It was introduced in 2002. Ten million of these units have been sold worldwide. We are seeing the application of robotics and related automated processes accelerating. Examining data from seventeen countries, Graetz and Michaels in 2015 observed that during the period 1993 to 2007 the use of robots had raised the growth rates of the countries surveyed by about 0.37 percentage points overall.[2] Robot density (robots per million hours worked) increased 150 percent, the nominal price of robots fell by half and the quality-adjusted price fell to one-fifth. The function of machine automation is to replace labour. The researchers found that unlike more general computer automation robots did not polarize the job market by shrinking mid-tier employment and expanding the low- and high-tiers. Rather factory robots reduced the hours of low-skilled employees and (to a lesser extent) mid-skilled employees and did not affect high-skilled workers. In 2013 industrial robot sales worldwide increased by 12 percent.[3] In countries like the United States, manufacturing moved offshore after 1970. It is now returning in the shape of high-tech peopleless factories. High-tech factory automation is not just happening in post-industrial nations. It is also occurring in China. Industrial China can no longer convince the generation born after 1990 to take factory jobs. They are not interested. Even in the world's factory, the machines are rising.

More striking still algorithmic and automated processes are replacing white-collar employment.[4] As with blue-collar technological unemployment this is not unprecedented. Office jobs have been automated before. Automatic teller machines, pioneered in the late 1960s, replaced bank teller jobs. What is new, though, is the scale of the looming change. Take the case of tax agents. The tax agent was a classic post-industrial mid-tier office occupation. After 1970, young people streamed into universities, took business degrees, exited with qualifications and became tax agents. At a conference in Sydney in 2014 the Australian Tax Office (ATO) warned tax agents that within 2 years Australian businesses would be able to report directly to the ATO every time that a sale or purchase was made, a payroll transaction occurred, or an employee was hired or fired — thus in principle eliminating most of the functions of the tax agent in preparing business activity statements and tax returns.[5] In other words algorithmic digitization makes possible large-scale disintermediation. In this case the service agent is replaced by machine–machine interaction: an industry business machine communicating with a tax office business machine, with data entered directly at the industry end.

Expect the tax agent example to be multiplied many times over in the coming decades. In an influential 2013 report, Carl Benedikt Frey and Michael A. Osborne estimated that 47 percent of US occupations had a significant probability of being reduced or eliminated by computerization.[6] The researchers looked in detail at 702 occupations. They compared occupational profile data from the US Bureau of Labor with studies of recent advances in machine learning and robotics as well as the prospect of offshoring (via the Internet) routine information-based tasks to lower-wage countries. In 2014, they applied their model to the United Kingdom. They concluded that 35 percent of contemporary jobs in the United Kingdom (and 30 percent of jobs in London) were at high risk of disappearing over the next decade as a result of computerization.[7] Jobs in sales, office and administrative support, services and management were notably vulnerable. The 'education, legal, community service, arts and media' cluster also showed vulnerabilities in spite of the common assumption that creative and social jobs defy automation. As it is the law and creative professions are already heavily computerized. The routine aspect of any computer-mediated role is liable eventually to be automated. One can also easily foresee the transfer of automated learning technologies into the regular classroom for teaching repetitive tasks like the times table or the periodic table.

Computerization is not a new process. As Frey and Osborne note, over past decades computers have already done away with the jobs of bookkeepers, cashiers and telephone operators. The economists Henry Sui and Nir Jaimovich observe that routine office and administrative support jobs have been declining since the 1980s.[8] The numbers of secretaries, bookkeepers, filing clerks, mail sorters and bank tellers have visibly shrunk. Automation and computing reduced demand for these white-collar occupations. From 1982 to 2012, routine occupations as a share of total US employment fell from 56 percent of employment to 44 percent. This structural shift became visible after the US recession of 1991 and again after the 2001 and 2009 recessions. The series of recessions during the second half of the post-industrial era repeatedly triggered reductions in routine occupations. As economic recovery occurred after each recession, the routine labour force did not return to its previous levels. In effect, computer capital began to replace repetitive labour.

As computers grow more sophisticated and (crucially) cheaper, computer capital increasingly supplants routine labour cohorts. To a significant extent already, personal assistants and secretaries have been replaced by mobile phones, digital assistants and personal computers. The decline in the real cost of large-scale computing services and robotic devices enables this substitution. It makes economic sense for employers to swap relatively expensive labour for cheaper computer or computer-controlled capital. The advances in computing mean that computers increasingly are able to replace labour where the tasks performed are repetitive and well-defined.[9] A well-defined task is one that is broken down into the most elementary parts, usually a series of steps. Repetition means repetition of the same set of steps. These are tasks that are in effect defined by procedures. In many cases these procedures branch. Such branching can be defined by programmable decision trees. Computer algorithms provide if-then rules for computing what to do. As automated decision tree systems grow in sophistication so does the range of tasks that become computable — enabling an ever-larger range of undertakings to be automated.

This means that automation is now extending into areas of employment such as driving a car through city traffic that previously were routine for human beings (most people can learn to drive a car) but seemingly impossible for robotic machinery. Some things that are routine for human beings such as recognizing handwritten letters still remain difficult for machines. But the scope of computerization in recent times has significantly expanded. This is due to advances in data mining, digital sensing, machine vision, computational statistics and AI. The result is that an increasing range of human tasks is being computerized and the pace of computerization is accelerating. A distinct intense wave or phase of automation is occurring. This accelerated phase extends roughly from 2006 when, after a lengthy period of disinterest, investors once again became interested in the potential applications of robotics in industry.[10]

In 2007, Bill Gates published an article in *Scientific American* predicting the coming of a new industry (aka robotics) that was comparable in nature to the personal computing industry that Gates pioneered in the 1980s. He envisaged a future world populated by robots doing laundry-folding, lawn-mowing, surveillance, floor-cleaning and food-and-medicine dispensing. We are some way away from a proficient laundry-folding robot but the rest are in use or nearly so. As Gates noted, it is no easy thing giving robots the kinds of capacities that human beings take for granted such as recognizing, grasping and navigating around objects. But he added that 'researchers are starting to find the answers' due to 'the increasing availability of tremendous amounts of computer power'. This power is still far from the capacity of the human brain but it is sufficient now to enable robots to do an expanding number of routine tasks.[11] The intersection of computing power with today's low-cost electronic sensors and the Global Position System has created a new technology spike. Like all such spikes, it is occurring on the back of decades of incremental development.

In its 2014 *London Futures* report, the consultancy firm Deloitte identified the kinds of jobs in London that have been significantly reduced already by automation in the 2001–13 period: library assistants and clerks, sales-related occupations, filing and record assistants and clerks, travel agents, counter clerks, PAs and secretaries, collectors and credit agents, pension and insurance clerks, account clerks and bookkeepers.[12] Worldwide across 2008–13, rising job types were iPhone developers, social media interns, data scientists, big data architects, cloud services specialists and digital marketers. Demand for high-end work continued to expand while demand for mid-tier office-and-sales jobs declined. The post-industrial era was an age of intermediation. It involved a big expansion of intermediate job layers and functions in medium-sized and large organizations. The auto-industrial era is removing these mid-tier jobs and roles. This is not just about technology. It also represents a cultural shift.

New technology creates jobs and eliminates jobs. The net result is what matters. Do the numbers of jobs created exceed the numbers of jobs eliminated — or not? The predictions of the 1970s were that computerization would cause a net reduction in the number of jobs. Mass technological unemployment would follow. That proved not to be true but it is just as interesting to understand why this was so. Job levels were sustained because government, education and health jobs expanded — or rather more precisely government, education and health bureaucracies expanded. Compliance became the post-industrial industry par excellence. Australia in 2014 had a GDP of $1,500 billion. It spent $250 billion on compliance — 15 percent of its GDP.[13] In other words, eight weeks of Australia's working year in 2014 was devoted to compliance activities. The effect of the post-industrial mania for compliance can be seen in American hospitals where today there is a minimum of 30 minutes paperwork for every hour of patient care.[14] A further 25 percent of costs are devoted to generic hospital administration. Is it any wonder that national healthcare costs are what they are?[15]

By replacing mid-tier office workers by machines auto-industrialism over the long term is likely to reverse the development of the post-industrial compliance society. Auto-industrialism replaces intermediation with disintermediation. It undoes the multiple layers of middle administration by automating them. Thus in place of an increasingly entropic intermedial society of bureaucratic agents, there are incipient signs of a move towards a society of auto-industrialized DIY autonomy. This is a society based on systems that eliminate non-essential functions, intermediaries and middle layers along with the repetitious duplicative semi-manual handling of data and the multiplication of make-work procedural steps that is typical of big government, big business and big altruism alike. It represents the opposite of the ethos of the post-modern, post-industrial era — and it signals the likely sharp reversal of trends that began in 1970. This shift will require a lot of social and political adjustment. The shift will also face a lot of resistance. Post-modern bureaucracy became socially addictive — and a powerful lobby for itself. The byzantine policy rules of the government-education-and-health sector are to it what customs barriers were to medieval dukedoms. They will not be readily dispensed with.

Disintermediation and algorithmic digitization are not in themselves new phenomena. They have already changed industries like the computer hardware business and the travel agent business. The difference today though is the impending scale, scope and pervasiveness of algorithmic change. According to Frey and Osborne, the occupational sectors most affected are in descending order of impact: Accommodation and Food Services, Transportation, Real Estate, Retail and Wholesale, Administrative and Support Services, Manufacturing, Construction, Finance and Insurance, and Mining. A predicted second tier of affected occupations includes: Arts, Entertainment and Recreation, Health Care and Social Assistance, Professional, Scientific, Technical Services, and Utilities.[16] Accordingly the scope of the impending change is broad and it touches a wide range of sectors and occupations across professional, office and manual work. All predictions of change are just that: predictions. These may or may not come to fruition. But equally it is clear that auto-industrial structural change has been taking place beneath the social surface at least since 1990. In that sense it is already a reality. It is reaching the point where the scale of the change is beginning to crystallize in a phase transition from a post-industrial to an auto-industrial economy.

What underscores this is the sheer number of industries, sectors and activities that are being transformed by auto-industrialization beginning with the military.[17]

Auto-industrialism is transforming the nature of warfare. There is increasing use of unmanned ground, marine and aerial vehicles for reconnaissance, transportation, mine clearance, surveillance and military strikes.[18] This is not just an effect of computing; rather it is computing combined with rapid advances in digital sensing. Auto-industrial technology is a merger of computing with large data storage and analytics and cheap sensor technology. By 2030 driverless taxis, cars and transport trucks will be common on the roads.[19] Given that human error is the major cause of road accidents, it is likely that a significant drop in road deaths and injuries will follow. Driverless transport trucks eventually will be integrated with robot factories and automated warehouses. Aeroplanes already are mostly piloted by computer systems except for take-off and landing.

The Hyatt hotel chain today is experimenting with automated check-in kiosks. Japan has developed a low-cost hotel model with robotized check-in, porter, cloakroom and concierge services.[20] China has installed thousands of robot noodle-makers in its restaurants. An integrated automated travel system of driverless taxis, ticketing, security checks, fast-food catering, gate control, piloting and hotel check-in is visible on the horizon. So is automated essay marking and robotic pick-and-pack in online shopping warehouses. The three-dimensional (3D) printing of buildings, which virtually eliminates building waste, and semi-automated factories manufacturing modular housing will significantly reduce housing costs. Warehouses with shelf-moving robots, automated harvesting robots, space probes, 'Longpen' remote signing and the motorized personal doppelgänger iPad Double are already with us. Robotic waste sorting systems and autonomous garbage disposal robots are being developed.[21] One-in-five lawn mowers now sold in Sweden are robot mowers.[22]

Just as auto-industrial technology combines computing with sensing and data analysis so auto-industrialization combines this hybrid technology with the disintermediation of industries. The propensity of the post-industrial era was to intermediate simply because its structure and growth relied so heavily on administration and compliance. This is beginning to be reversed. Disintermediation is extending into industries ranging from taxis, clothes and fashion to car purchases and beverages. Forty years ago consumers would have resisted this but the near-pervasive experience of human–machine interaction in personal computing in advanced economies today makes dealing with automated systems familiar and often preferable.[23] Small children now walk up to the lounge room TV set and try and swipe it as if it was a tablet computer. Even industries that at first glance might seem unlikely to be affected will be: household consumers today who produce their own energy are disintermediating the electric utility industry. Television networks were classic post-industrial age intermedial organizations. They purchased programs, scheduled the programs for view-ers and broadcast them. The television audience today is decreasing and it is rapidly aging. Viewers increasingly schedule their own viewing. They started with DVDs. They are now streaming downloads from providers like Netflix and Amazon who in turn are becoming television and film production houses.

In 2015 the city of Seattle increased the minimum wage to $15 an hour. Progressive opinion, which dominates that city, rejoiced. Understandably the city's restaurants were less thrilled as they spend 35 percent of their income on labour. Some simply shut up shop; others raised prices, putting the squeeze on their low-income customers. However, the most notable response came from operators who adapted — with technology. They replaced labour with machines. The future of fast food given this scenario is ordering from machines at the counter or from tablet computers installed on tables. But surely custom-ers want the personal touch? The rise of online sales suggests that this is not so. In fact high levels of impersonal public interaction correlate strongly with societies that have high levels of creativity and productivity and with no obvi-ous cost to personal intimacy, if anything the converse.[24] As it expanded in the 1970s, industrial automation replaced high-wage skilled industrial labour. A lot of service work and manual labour, though, was immune to automation. This is less the case today. Until recently it has been difficult to program robots for manual work away from the factory line where tasks and environments are inconstant. Robots still find tasks like folding towels difficult to do. But their manual dexterity is increasing. Sensing and mimetic technologies are improv-ing robotic motor skills. And, ironically, while the true humanoid robot lies in the distant future, advances in exoskeletal technologies are starting to bring the robotoid human being to reality.[25]

The looming impact of automation is not just on service or manual work. Today computer programs exist that automate the production of low-level news reporting.[26] These provide automated reporting of stock movements and sports data. Robo-news processes already produce millions of items a year. There is no way to tell the difference between these automated reports and human writing. Computers though do not just automate. They also facilitate the prosumer — that is, the consumer who produces. Until around the year 2000 the production of media content was dominated by professionals. In the past decade, we have seen the re-emergence of the skilled and semi-skilled amateur. This phenomenon is reminiscent of the nineteenth century. It is worth remembering that, until the twentieth century, much of the best science and philosophy was produced by gifted amateurs rather than professionals. We appear to be trending back in this direction.

Take the case of photography. Until recently, the field of photography had a core of professional photographers. Digital cameras in digital phones in an instant changed that. Today 2.5 billion people own digital cameras; more photos are taken today every two minutes than were taken in the whole of the nineteenth century. In 2013 Facebook's Instagram service (one of many cloud storage archives) had 150 million users and 16 billion photos. In 2012, when it was purchased by Facebook for $1 billion in cash and stock, Instagram had 13 employees. In 2014 Facebook, with 1.4 billion active users, had 7,000 employees. The pre-digital photo giant Kodak at its height employed nearly 150,000 people directly and many more indirectly through its distribution networks.[27] Instagram's distribution is automated through the Internet. It is a prosumer-dominated entity. Those who consume its contents produce its contents. Newspapers also were once big employers but no longer. A third of the workforce and a half of the mastheads have disappeared in the past decade. Much news-related content is now created by amateurs in a DIY landscape of podcasts, tweets, blogs, online magazines, video clips, news aggregators and prosumers.[28]

FUTURE JOBS

Often it is assumed that healthcare employment will grow in the future due to aging populations. This is true to a degree. However, even in this field automation will be felt and perhaps more than is conventionally expected. In 2015, the US Bureau of Labor Statistics (BLS) reported that personal care aides were the fastest growing US occupational group, numbering 1,190,000, with median earnings of $19,000 a year. No qualification was required for these jobs though most aides had a high school diploma. Half of all personal care aides worked full-time. Frey and Osborne predict there is a 74 percent probability that these jobs will be computerized.[29] Robot-assisted aged care and robot-assisted surgery, including remote surgery, are developing. Robots that lift, feed, bathe and motor the aged are being designed along with self-monitoring health technologies. Advances in automated sensing technologies have produced computer applications for digital phones enabling DIY blood oxygen monitoring, electrocardiograms, dermatoscopy (examination of skin lesions), otoscopy (ear examinations), blood glucose readings, lung breath analysis, blood pressure monitoring, ultrasounds, slit lamp eye examinations and (soon) brain scanning. Smartphone applications are extending into areas of spectrometry (optical analysis of the wavelengths of molecules) and drug screening.

Without removing the need for medical diagnosis and expert interpretation, the technology markedly expands the scope for the self-management of conditions. In a medicalized world where routine testing is a major cost factor, home testing and self-reporting offer significant potential time-and-cost benefits especially for patients with chronic conditions. Responsible self-monitoring of an individual's health is an essential component of a well-ordered self-managed society. Just as the Internet became a library without librarians, the auto-industrial society promises expert healthcare while reducing the scale and cost of intermediation.

The health sector was a key post-industrial employer. It grew rapidly. As with education, health acquired an aura of unquestionability during the post-industrial era. It became a sanctified public good. This combined with the fact of aging populations in major economies lent its continued expansion the impression of apparent inevitability. Yet like all economic segments in modern society the health sector is ultimately susceptible to industrialization. Thus it is easy to assume that health jobs will not be affected by automation when in fact they will be. The American economist David Autor pioneered the study of the shrinkage of mid-skill jobs in advanced economies. Yet even as recently as 2012, he cited radiology technicians, phlebotomists and nurse technicians as examples of currently expanding mid-skill jobs likely to survive the intensifying wave of automation.[30] Current technology advances suggest otherwise.

The Stanford-based company Veebot is developing a robotic venipuncture system.[31] Robots are being developed not only for interpretative but also interventional radiology (procedures involving the entry of body cavities).[32] Panasonic's HOSPI-R, an autonomous delivery robot, has been designed to transport drugs so nurses and technicians do not have to do the task. Current technology development points to a substantial replacement of skilled and semi-skilled labour in hospitals in the foreseeable mid-term. General Electric is developing a robot system to locate, sort, sterilize and deliver surgical tools;[33] I-Sur is working on a system to automate basic surgical procedures like puncturing, cutting and suturing.[34] ABUS is an algorithmically driven ultrasound system that automates the breast imaging process; RxRobots' humanoid machines coach children in pain control techniques. A robot is being developed to remove objects from the digestive system like batteries that have been accidentally swallowed.[35] Today there is the increasing installation of robotic pick-and-pull systems to locate, prepare, package and deliver hospital pharmaceuticals along with the growing use by doctors of computerized clinical decision support systems that apply if-then rules to patient data.[36]

According to the US BLS, in 2014 the top four out of the six highest paid, fastest growing occupations in the United States were health-related. This reflects the classic, mature, post-industrial social model. This model privileged government, health and education employment. In 2014, the highest growth occupations in the United States included postgraduate qualified postsecondary specialist health teachers, nurse practitioners, physical therapists and physician assistants. Health also dominated the next income tier, with demand for genetic counsellors, post-secondary nursing instructors, diagnostic medical sonographers, audiologists and dental hygienists growing rapidly. Not far behind these in occupational demand were various kinds of medical technologists: magnetic resonance imaging technologists and nuclear medicine technologists. It is only then that a different set of occupations begins to show up: geographers, cartographers and photogrammetrists, cost estimators, web developers, personal financial advisors, operations research analysts and logisticians.

Of these various occupations, which ones will be at least partially displaced by robots? In 2013, Frey and Osborne ranked occupations according to their probability of computerization — from the least likely to the most likely to be computerized.[37] Based on these projections, the chances of the 2014-era, fast-growing, high-paying jobs being automated are as follows: cartographers and photogrammetrists (88 percent), dental hygienists (68 percent), personal financial advisors (58 percent), cost estimators (57 percent), diagnostic medical sonographers (35 percent), geographers (25 percent), web developers (21 percent), physician assistants (14 percent), nuclear medicine technologists (13 percent), physical therapists (2 percent), operations research analysts (3.5 percent), counsellors (negligible), audiologists (negligible), logisticians (negligible) and teachers and instructors (negligible).

As is to be expected, automation has variable effects. Some are deep-going, others are minimal or non-existent. The signs of medical automation are significant. On the other hand whether teachers and counsellors will be as immune from industrialization as Frey and Osborne suggest is an interesting question. Education was the most sacred totem of the post-industrial era, even more so than the health sector. How much of this pseudo-sacred aura also shapes predictions about the future of education is unclear. Arguably automated and semi-automated learning systems will be considerably more commonplace in the future than Frey and Osborne predict.[38] This is simply because a considerable part of learning, instruction and assessment is repetitive in nature. The strengths of digital learning technologies lie in the provision of routine assessment and feedback, low-level repetitive explanation, and instant, out-of-hours and on-demand feedback.[39] In 2016, a Georgia Tech professor employed seven teaching assistants. One of them, it turned out, was an AI bot. No one noticed the difference.[40] The bot was programmed on the basis of only giving answers that had a 97 percent probability of being correct. This is possible to do because much of an assistant's work is routine and repetitive.

Despite its self-image, the daily work of higher education in fact is filled with repetition.[41] Marking, baseline explication and delivery are weighed down with duplication and reiteration. The repeat lecture year-on-year is a classic example. On-demand streamed online video delivery of lectures in place of the traditional classroom lecture is for that reason very efficient. In addition it frees students from having to attend class at a scheduled time and place. Further, its composed nature and infographic potentials allow a much greater quantity of information per minute to be delivered by the lecturer.

In short in the auto-industrial age, many current job types will wither or disappear. The automating of jobs is the norm of industrial societies. That is what happened to agricultural and then manufacturing occupations. It is now happening to service, office, government, health and education work. All economic sectors in an industrial society are ultimately susceptible to automation. That is what makes an industrial society an industrial society. Eventually in any sector, routine operations will be identified, analysed, programmed and turned over to machines. The human response to this invariably is that 'a machine cannot replace what I do, because what I do is not routine. It requires judgment, intuition and creativity'. Sometimes this is true; often it is not. The human delusion is to think that a job that is routine is unpredictable; that a knowledge of rules is the same as the exercise of judgement; or that calling a job 'professional' or 'skilled' means that it involves unprogrammable intuition or imagination.

Does this mean then that the coming of the auto-industrial society will be one of high unemployment, high underemployment, less opportunity and less mobility? This is possible. It cannot be excluded. However, in the past two hundred years, the most advanced economies have seen artisan production, agriculture and manufacturing mechanized and automated. Will service, office, government, health and education jobs go the same way? Yes. The notion that there is a 'post-industrial' space in an industrial society that is immune from automation is an illusion. The big government and big corporate sectors in the mid-twentieth century saw themselves as the wave of the future. Now that future is automating them.

As these sectors shrink, what will take their place? That is unpredictable. No one can answer that question in the same way that in 1970 no one could look into a crystal ball and say 'these will be the jobs in 1990s'. Job types are constantly being created and destroyed. Consequently it is not possible to project with certainty the net employment consequences of any technology wave. We do not know with any assurance what new industries will arise and to what degree these industries will substitute for employment losses as established industries shrink. It is a mistake to project current trends in a linear fashion into the future. What is certain though is that many kinds of repeating tasks that human beings currently do will be automated in the future. That is not peculiar to auto-industrialism. Rather it is nature of industrialism, past and future. That means occupations related to those tasks will shrink and are already shrinking.

The mantra of the post-industrial era was that good jobs required degrees. This is much less evidently true of the emerging auto-industrial era. The US BLS classifies most jobs according to the level of qualification required for them. Breaking the BLS 2012–22 projection of US high-growth occupations down by qualification requirement, the resulting data shows that 1 percent of these projected employees will require some college, 10 percent an associate degree, 17 percent a bachelor's degree, 6 percent a master's degree, 12 percent a doctoral or professional degree, 31 percent a high school diploma, 15 percent less than high school and 8 percent a training certificate.[42] Currently, 12 percent of Americans have less than high school, 30 percent graduate high school, 19 percent have some college, 10 percent an associate degree, 18 percent a bachelor's degree, 7 percent a master's degree and 3 percent a professional or doctoral degree.[43] Possession of qualifications among the current US population across *all* age cohorts over 18 roughly equates the projected labour force needs. Yet in sharp contrast, the current level of enrolment of 18–24-year-olds in higher education is significantly out of kilter with projected labour force needs. Today, 41 percent of 18–24-year-old Americans are enrolled in 2-year and 4-year degree programs (13 percent and 28 percent of the age cohort respectively).[44] Post-industrial lobbies incessantly pressed for the expansion of higher education after 1970. The result is that today's 28 percent of 19-year-olds in a 4-year college is at odds with the 17 percent of employees in high-growth occupations who (foreseeably) will need a 4-year bachelor's degree. Even today's 2-year colleges are oversubscribed. With the incipient decline of mid-tier jobs, so goes the demand for mid-tier qualifications. The auto-industrial age favours academic polarization: at one end, advanced degrees; at the other end, high school diplomas or less. In short, relatively fewer of the expanding jobs of the near future will require 4-year degrees.[45] Universities will enrol fewer not more undergraduate students per capita. Notably between 2010 and 2015 higher education enrolment in the United States dropped 13 percent.[46]

While the demand for mid-tier credentialed labour is in decline, demand for two other types of labour appears to be increasing. One is for dexterous manual or technical labour that is not easy to replace with a machine. Any kind of manual or technical labour where a person works in a predictable mappable position doing repeating tasks is apt to be replaced by a machine. At the same time demand for dexterous manual or technical labour requiring actions that are responsive to subtle, unique, unpredictable, non-routinized or rapidly changing human needs seems likely to increase. Something similar applies to the 'personal care–healthcare' segment of advanced economies. Contemporary demand for care is driven by populations that are living longer. However, as previously noted, the care workforce is by no means immune from automation. Accordingly, current projections for high-growth healthcare occupations may well underestimate the degree to which machines will substitute for human beings carrying out routine care functions, including in the home, by 2025. On the other hand it is also plausible that the non-routine care economy will expand. The semantic emphasis here is less on 'care' and more on the 'non-routine' component of care. It is difficult to predict the net result of declining routine work and possibly increasing demand for non-routine kinds of care or what those might be or even how they might be defined.

The nature of the 'non-routine' ranges from work that has an unpredictable aspect to work that has a 'creative' aspect. It captures a spectrum of activity that requires varying degrees of initiative and problem solving. The capacity of the home health aide or the physical therapy assistant to figure out when a patient wants help, does not want it, does not need it and should not be given it, is a subtle exercise in everyday judgement. It is not possible to reduce such judgement to a rule. Judgement requires a certain amount of imagination: that is, the ability to see oneself as another; to imagine what pain means not to the happy person that you are but to the unhappy person who is sitting in front of you. Such judgement falls short of creativity in the strict sense but it nonetheless requires degrees of problem solving, adaptability and resourcefulness.

INTELLIGENCE VERSUS IMAGINATION

One thing is clear: labour that is algorithmic in nature can be replaced by machines. This is true in principle. Increasingly in practice such labour is being replaced by automata of various kinds. An algorithm is a set of unambiguous instructions to perform a series of actions in a prescribed step-like sequence to achieve a goal. The non-routine component of labour is that which cannot be reduced to unambiguous instructions. It is the aspect of work that involves initiative, judgement and imagination.

To better understand the difference between algorithmic machine intelligence and the creative human imagination, consider the case of David Cope, a music professor, now retired, at the University of California at Santa Cruz.[47]

He devised computer programs that produce facsimiles of the music of Bach, Vivaldi, Beethoven, Chopin, Mahler and Scott Joplin. His speciality is algorithmic composition. Yet this is composition only in a limited sense. Cope divides a composer's work into stylistic units and provides programming instructions for their recombination by the computer. That is not creation; rather it is the reverse engineering of the act of creation. People who create a lot recognize this procedure. Creators have standard stylistic units that they combine in typical ways. This is a shortcut to creation. It is an aid to productivity. But it is not (in itself) creation. Cope's algorithmic music, readily available on YouTube, is recognizably 'in the style of' Bach or Mahler, and so on. But instructively, like all works 'in the style of', these hold our attention only for a brief moment. In other words, they do not 'capture' our imagination. It is important to try and understand why not. Cope's algorithmic compositions are flat, soulless and despirited. They are proficient academic works perhaps but they lack the crucial creative element of surprise. As you might expect of a computer program they are formulaic. Their interest value lies in the creativity of the computer programming but not in the work produced.

That said we do not always want the world to be surprising. I want my toothbrush to be in the same place every morning. Much of life repeats. Repetition is the basis of ritual, which human beings find attractive. Everyday repetition means that the same routine is carried out following the same steps in a given sequence depending on initial conditions. An algorithm is much the same. An algorithm allows the statement: *if* the stylistic unit L is completed *then* follow it with unit G or unit T depending on the circumstances N or M. So *if* L is complete and the state N exists *then* do G. The 'if-then' sequence is a foundation of logic and the basis of computable progressions. It also structures repetitive everyday decision making. Yet life and work do not always follow 'if-then' sequences. The most compelling music follows a predictable sequence but then breaks the sequence and yet does so in a difficult-to-define, interesting way. The break that occurs is satisfying in the way that predictable sequencing is and yet it is unpredictable (and thereby heightens the satisfaction of the work). The predictable but surprising sequence does not follow an 'if-then' pattern yet it is not the anarchic opposite of this either. It breathes life into routine by departing from it in a way that captures a higher, more daring order of things. It defies expectation yet in doing so creates a higher expectation that will itself eventually be translated into routines that can be programmed into a machine. But we cannot program pleasing aesthetic surprise into a machine. Just as there is no rubric, rule, standard, routine, or repetition that we can institute that will make a person creative.

Consider the aspiration of robotics engineers to achieve a human-like artificial intelligence. This aspiration came about because of an interesting creative leap that occurred in the 1950s. This was the idea that machines could be ('as if') intelligent. Creativity couples that which stands apart.[48] In making the creative leap that combined the idea of the machine and the idea of intelligence, AI researchers also unwittingly revealed the limits of the concept of intelligence — at least in its dominant twentieth-century form. The idea of intelligence was popularized by progressive intellectuals in the early twentieth century.[49] They placed their faith in intelligence.[50] The word became a hallmark of American progressive ideology and its influential education ideas. It was a term of self-approbation for progressive intellectuals who looked on their own philosophies and policies as the acme of intelligence.[51] Those who disagreed with this — notably conservatives — were (by definition) unintelligent and the epitome of stupidity.

The progressive movement's defining early intellectual peak occurs in the work of John Dewey. Dewey uses the term intelligence obsessively. Yet it turns out that intelligence was far from the crowning cognitive ability that its advocates supposed it to be. The growth of AI and its increasing applications in everyday life, not least its job-replacing applications, indicates that the nature of intelligence is rather less special than its small army of proponents insisted it was.

Intelligence was defined as the via media of progress. A century ago, progressive intellectuals waved away the ideas of finality, limits, boundaries, conclusions and permanent forms. Dewey wrote millions of words saying in effect that the ancient Greeks were wrong in admiring permanent things.[52] The durable symmetries, boundaries, cycles, waves and proportions of nature and beauty, he argued, were secondary to things that change. Intelligent beings accordingly think first about contingent ends-in-view. They cogitate on the means of achieving those goals. They move from one end-in-view (having achieved it) to the next end-in-view. In that way, they progress. Progress is an effect of planning and plans are 'if-then' sequences. For example, 'if I allocate resource A and person B, then task C can be carried out'. Anyone familiar for example with university plans knows though that that never actually happens.[53] Post-industrial universities are like the old Soviet Union. Plans are the necessary delusion of their being. Thus while the collapse of Communism definitively proved the failure of the idea of planning this did nothing to stop the relentless growth of the all-administrative state and the all-administrative university in democratic societies. This is because progress, the *sine qua non* of democratic life of the past century, rules out boundaries, limits, cycles, consummations and finalities. That is to say, it cannot stop whatever it starts. Intelligence without reference to the durable forms of nature and beauty has no resting point.

The ironic coda to this story is that auto-industrial society is now systematically automating intelligence. It is programming intelligence into machines. A century of the idolization of intelligence culminated in the post-modern knowledge societies. The rampant bureaucracies of those societies are now beginning to be replaced by machines. What you cannot program into a machine, however, is imagination. You cannot program a Cézanne who imagined landscape as solid geometry and solid rocks as liquid pouring down from the hills he painted or a Niels Bohr who imagined physical waves as particles. Such intellectual complementarity is the work of the imagination. Accordingly, the component of work that we call intelligence increasingly is being programmed into machines while imagination is necessarily exempted from this.

Take the example of computer-controlled additive manufacturing, an auto-industrial age technology. What this kind of boutique manufacturing requires are not production line workers as adjuncts to machines or office workers to process employee benefits. Rather the key employees are those who design the geometrically sophisticated 3D print objects. The designer needs to know how to operate CAD and STL computer programs but ultimately the intellectual and economic value that is produced lies in the design and ingenuity of the objects produced. Design takes the known forms of nature and beauty and reworks them imaginatively, that is surprisingly. This bias towards imagination rather than intelligence is markedly different from the bias that was built into post-industrial credentialed labour. Accordingly, many of the ideas about work and education that came into vogue after 1970 offer little guidance for the auto-industrial age. The conventional mass university degree for example is practically useless. At the same time, though, we understand very little about the faculty of the imagination even though we rely increasingly on that faculty. I can list on the fingers of my two hands almost all the authors who have had anything interesting to say about the imagination — from Hazlitt to Kant and Coleridge to Castoriadis. What I can tell you is that the imagination is not programmable. The imagination cannot be coded. It cannot be reduced to unambiguous instructions. It does not follow an 'if-then' pattern. Making jokes is a good model of the imagination.[54] A joke supposes we can quickly recognize one thing 'as if' it was something else altogether. The faculty of the imagination allows us to look at an inkjet printer and think, well, one day I can imagine a print machine printing out foodstuffs.[55] Inspired science fiction writers have these kinds of thoughts; so do inventive technologists.

When well-meaning writers on the economic future say that creative work will survive the coming of the machines, this though raises the question: how many of us are actually creative? The answer possibly is: fewer than you may think. I do not mean: how many of us have a genius for creation? The answer to that question by definition is: not many. Rather I am asking: how many people in everyday work and life show themselves to be regularly creative in modest but meaningful ways? The answer arguably is: not so many. That may or may not be correct. But it does raise a warning: if more and more routine work is automated, we can be reasonably sure that 'creative' occupations will survive the rise of the machines. But it remains an open question how many such occupations there will be.

The promise of post-industrial mass higher education was in essence a fraud. It was a form of social self-delusion. The idea of 'mass creativity' is likewise nonsensical. At the same time, the vision of a jobless neo-patrimonial society carved up between wealthy elites and a minimum-income mass is detestable. So what then is the functional alternative to post-industrialism and neo-patrimonialism? It might be called a problem-solving society. Problem solving is a kind of demotic resourcefulness. It is illustrated in the difference between the hotel clerk who repeatedly checks in an endless flow of guests and the one who fixes the problem when your hotel *Wi-Fi* fails to work for the umpteenth time. As the machines eventually take over the check-in desk and eventually the folding of hotel towels, what is the future (if any) of the hotel industry workforce? It depends ultimately on what hotel owners and users in the future imagine a hotel to be. Will it be simply a proficient automated staffless version of the rest-sleep-eat-exercise formula that exists today, or will staff still be employed, not to apply the formulas that make up the entry-stay-and-exit sequence but rather to solve the unexpected problems of the guests — 'there are no trouser hangers left in the wardrobe; the tap in the bathroom is dripping; I'm late, how do I get to the airport?'.

Problem solving runs through the human experience. A machine cannot solve problems. Problem solving requires us to do 'imaginative' things that machines cannot do such as change perspective on a problem; visualize, model or simulate it; define the problem analogically; redefine the problem analogically; compare situations where the problem occurs and where it does not occur and draw inferences from that. These methods are all practical applications of the human imagination that allows us to see X as if it is not-X. A problem-solving workforce would be distinctly different in character from the rule-based-team-process workforce typical of the post-industrial age. A problem-solving workforce does not exist (yet). There is no reason that it should or will exist excepting for human desire and need. But its hypothetical existence does at least answer the question: what kind of value do human beings create that machines cannot? If you answer that question, you start to answer the question: what kinds of occupations will survive in the auto-industrial age?[56]

PATTERN WORK

When John Dewey declared that the ancient Greeks were wrong in admiring permanent things — the forms, patterns, symmetries, boundaries, cycles, waves and proportions of nature and beauty — he set the tone and agenda for twentieth-century mass industrialism and post-industrialism. These worldviews emphasized change in place of durability and process in place of pattern. This was a world of large companies and big government. Qualities of grace and beauty, truth and loveliness were downplayed. The prevailing ethos of the time was fascinated by the tensions between certainty and contingency, assurance and exigency and the ways these were reconciled. Procedure was played off against progress only to become identical with progress. But beneath the surface of the mass-industrial and post-industrial societies the older and deeper values of form and figure persisted. They resisted the concerted attempt to sweep them aside. They lived on often in surprising ways.

Institutional high art largely disowned them. But not so everyday aesthetics. In the century between 1910 and 2010 the aesthetics of everyday life quietly emerged as an economic force. Consider today the case of broadcast television. It is crowded with home renovation and home purchase reality programs. These programs stimulate a taste for DIY aestheticized construction. The impulse underlying this is archaic. The desire to embellish everyday surfaces is set deep in both the human psyche and humankind's most creative societies. Tiled surfaces with intricate decoration reach back to the ancient civilization of Mesopotamia. They are an expression of humanity's civilizing impulse. In decorative tiling, art, science, economics and urbanism intersect. In 2013 Americans consumed $2.4 billion worth of ceramic tile. In the United States in 2011, art museums in their entirety produced in contrast only $1.5 billion of economic value.[57]

Today the Design Robotics Group in the Graduate Design School at Harvard University is developing the 3D printing of ceramic tiles. The element that 3D printing or additive manufacturing offers is the customization of production. The 3D print process is efficient for short production runs, prototyping and personalized production. This points to one of the likely job generators of auto-industrial societies. These are design-fuelled businesses that merge design and technology to produce customized short-run high-value products that have a significant design component and an aura that derives from the short run.[58] This is a kind of art-industrialism where economics, atmosphere, form and technology merge into one. The technology is automated, computer-controlled and algorithmically precise. The high-value part of the work lies in the design component and the intricate coordination of design, technology and business. These aspects rely more on the 'as if' than the 'if-then' cognitive faculty.

Design in the auto-industrial age is not a species of studio art or the fine arts. The age of the public art gallery began in the late eighteenth century. It reached a blockbuster-fuelled late peak at the end of the twentieth century. From the Uffizi Gallery in eighteenth-century Florence to the Guggenheim Museum in twentieth-century Bilbao, the public gallery was a status institution. While much of modern life shifted from status to contract, the gallery staunchly remained a domain based on rank distinctions. It is dedicated to things that are 'high' as opposed to things that are 'low'. The prestige of the modern art institution is in part explained by the fact that it took over from the church a consecrated or hallowed status. Galleries consequently possess a quasi-sacred aura. They attract modern 'pilgrims' and anchor large visitor economies. In contrast industrialized reproduction, mechanical and later electronic, represent a different arc of influence.

Reproduced objects cannot be exclusive in any sense and thus they cannot be deified as original. They lack eminence, reputation or high status. They lack an aura. They do not belong in an exclusive space. Rather they are demonstrably demotic. They are widely available. They owe as much to science and technology as they do to art or the arts.[59] Their model is more Saturday shopping than Sunday worship. Yet even though it is not sacral, the power of consumer aesthetics still draws on the traditional power of beauty. Sometimes this power fails and we end up with kitsch or bad taste. But equally, high or sacral institutions also fail when they become academic. We have loud, cheap and cheesy on the one hand to contend with; on the other hand pedantry, snobbishness and insipidness.

The power of beauty rests heavily on the indomitable allure of pattern. There is some reason to think that the diminishing amount of knowledge work of the post-industrial period eventually will be replaced in part by pattern work. New flexible machines are arising that will transform areas like engineering and house construction. There are prototypes of automated machines today that can lay bricks and construct the shell of a house in a matter of hours. A 3D machine exists that can print a steel bridge.[60] Peopleless factories can produce engineered timbers to precise specifications and prefabricate building modules for rapid on-site erection. Such machines replace labour. Yet they do more than this. They also present new possibilities. Computer-controlled machines

can engineer buildings and building parts using hitherto unexploited geom-
etries and pattern-forms. One way of thinking about pattern work is 'design'.
Computer-controlled machines significantly expand the possibilities of design-
based work not just in areas that we conventionally think of as related to design
like buildings but rather across the broad gamut of human occupation.

Pattern work is expansive. It is a different way of conceptualizing activities and industries. It points us away from the post-industrial notion of work
as involving the manipulation of signs and symbols.[61] It conceptualizes work
as involving the use of shape and configuration. Ratios, power laws, curves,
cycles, morphologies, symmetries, branches, skeletal structures, waves, fractals, ripples, tiles, check-boards, spirals and bubbles are the imagistic basis for
this kind of productive human action.[62] The 'shape of things' is the insignia of
an emerging world where language, semiotics, signals, symbols, gestures and
marks — the key self-referential anchors of the post-industrial era — are no
longer the leading generators of meaning.

Pattern work is different from pattern recognition. Computers can do the
latter and do so with increasing competence. Pattern work rather resembles
the following: when early commercial airports were being constructed, architects had to design arrivals-and-departures areas. The design that was widely
adopted was akin to an aircraft hangar — a vast towering barn-like space. The
cognitive medium for this kind of pattern work was analogy. The human mind
is analogical.[63] That is the way it creates.[64] Computers are not analogical. The
cognitive scientist Douglas Hofstadter broke with the AI research community
over the question of the centrality of analogy to intelligence.[65] The efforts of
his graduate students to create analogical computer software programs have
not been especially fruitful. Computers that (like the human brain) can create
new forms by analogy with existing patterns do not exist. An automated brick-
laying machine can already lay down almost three times the number of bricks
that a manual labourer can.[66] In the not-too-distant future, most commercial
brick-laying will be done by machines. But a machine cannot look at the ripples
of the sea or sand and imagine a dwelling where the bricks are laid out in a
ripple pattern. Engineered computer-controlled factory and robotic construction methods, as well as 3D print methods of construction, open up an untold
array of geometric design possibilities. Repetitive work such as routine bricklay-
ing will shrink. But pattern work will increase as the technological possibilities
for the manipulation of patterns grow.

It is difficult to predict the impact of this on labour markets. Creative work
in the strict sense has never been more than a tiny portion of human labour.
As it is starting to become clear, knowledge work was not very creative.

Machines are now replacing knowledge workers. To what extent this will be matched by an increased demand for pattern work cannot be foreseen. Design is one of the rare areas of middle-class, mid-tier income that has grown in the past decade or so.[67] One should be wary of romanticizing or exaggerating this. That said, though, if we look back over the past century we see an incremental, steady and non-trivial growth of aesthetics in everyday life. This is true of white goods, consumer durables, food consumption, housing and urban development. This phenomenon is also mirrored in business. Today the most successful start-up businesses concentrate on product design.[68] They rent everything else (manufacturing, logistics, marketing) from third parties.

Design is a proxy for the imagination. The importance of the cognitive faculty of the imagination expands in advanced auto-industrial economies. Imagination is the cerebral power that generates the kind of inventive supply of intriguing objects, processes and experiences that animate high-functioning economies and in so doing generates growth and prosperity. Imagination is the cognitive top tier of a set of mental faculties that cascade downward through figuring, reckoning, surmising, conjecturing and hypothesizing to prudence, judgement and foresight. All look at 'what is not there' in terms of 'what is there' and analogize between the two. Design accordingly is an example of something larger. Work in the auto-industrial age arguably will not be dominated by knowledge work but rather by analogical work. This is work that relies on the everyday human cognitive capacity to draw analogies or likenesses. Where post-industrial knowledge work was analytical, compartmental, procedural and well-defined, auto-industrial work is less well defined and more analogical. It relies on parallels, correspondences, correlations and comparisons. The designer looks at a blank screen and begins by thinking 'perhaps something like...'. This is work that a machine cannot do. It is work that relies on the cognitive processes of resemblance, likeness, similitude and similarity.

This is not just 'aesthetic' work by any means. The economist Tyler Cowen has made the point that as knowledge work declines, the demand for character work is increasing.[69] Employers are less and less interested in hiring persons for their qualifications (when everyone has a qualification, qualifications are valueless). Instead, they want persons who are reliable, trustworthy and have other valuable character traits. Character is closely related to judgement. As early as Aristotle it was understood that character traits were general in nature and so had to be applied to situations. Thus a reliable person has to figure out how to be reliable in a given circumstance. People figure these things out analogically. Take the example of the former student who in high school reliably handed assignments in on time. At work that same individual reasons by analogy — and figures out how to meet work deadlines or the demands of the daily starting time schedule.

Character is a measure of reliability and dedication. Its conceptual roots lie in the classical and Christian world of Aristotle, Aquinas and Calvin. What happened to character is a bit like what happened to religion. It was de-institutionalized. Universities removed character tests (like regular attendance at chapel) from the curriculum in the late nineteenth century as modern culture became 'secularized'. Secularization though is something of a misnomer for the process of religious de-institutionalization. In modernity churches have shrunk in significance. Yet religious concepts like redemption, perdition, evil and faithfulness continue to circulate in the general culture — through literature and art. Major societies today may be outwardly irreligious but inwardly, culturally, they are still far from irreligious. We see this in the world of work. The credentialed worker is increasingly less employable today. Yet the faithful worker, the one who can meet a deadline and who is reliable, steady and productive, has an increasing chance of being employed.

It is often said that work of a social nature will survive automation. Care workers, social workers and teachers are typically cited in this connection. But the contention is misleading. Work that involves interaction with other persons is not immune to automation. It is unlikely that fast food counter staff will survive automated screen ordering.[70] The reason is that the social interaction of counter staff with customers does not rely on analogical judgement. Staff do not regularly have to ask themselves: *what do I do in this situation*? Their role is minutely defined and repetitive. The work of an athletic trainer, occupational therapist, marriage counsellor, fundraiser or musical director is 'social' in a different way. It involves lots of interaction with others but it is less the nominally social aspect of these jobs that resists automation and more that each interaction relies heavily on analogical reasoning. Every athlete, patient, couple in crisis, beneficiary or performance ensemble is different — and yet resembles others. Thus patient A has to be likened to type X. The similarity of the performance of athlete B or quartet C to past examples N and M has to be considered — and accepted or dismissed. In other words, these are roles that rely heavily on judgement.

We often say about buildings that we like them because they have 'character'. This is true even of new buildings. The 'character' of these works is a function of their good composition. A work that is well designed or well formed is one that is evidently created to last. It has the stamp of character (meaning durability). It also has the idiosyncrasy of character in the same way that we think of someone who is 'a character'. This person is not like everyone else but rather stands out, apart, in interesting ways. Computer programs do not have character. That is an attribute of their function. They do grunt work, in great volumes, ceaselessly. They are entities without souls. We do not need them to have a soul — for much work is soulless. We are pleased that machines do such work. Yet we are also often displeased at the same time. This is because we think that if human beings do not have drudge work to do then there is no guarantee that they will find a job. This prospect causes social anxiety.

Over the past century our institutions became increasingly soulless. The age of the organization was hostile to character. The universities are a good example of this. At one time they had plenty of room for idiosyncratic and unusual persons. This is no longer the case. The post-modern mass bureaucratic university turned itself into a machine for compliance.[71] The irony is that, as a consequence, the post-modern university is fated to shrink in size and influence in the auto-industrial age. There are simply better machines for compliance. Programmable machines will take over simple routines and algorithmic procedures. In occupations that do flourish in the auto-industrial age, character will replace compliance. The future will rely more on those who are able to act on their own initiative in performing everyday tasks. These are persons who can reliably undertake duties that are not rule-governed or unambiguous. These are the kinds of tasks that require judgement even if only in the most elementary sense. Situational imagination, prudence and perceptiveness become key in an auto-industrial world in which most routine functions have been automated.

QUALIFICATIONS NOT REQUIRED

When the management consultancy firm Deloitte in 2014 asked London employers what skills they increasingly require for their businesses, the top responses were: digital know-how, management, creativity, entrepreneurship, problem solving and negotiation.[72] Less important than any of those matters was the factor of qualifications. Here we see the nub of the problem that faces the universities in the auto-industrial era. As it emerged after 1970 the mass university was designed to produce a post-industrial white-collar workforce. The demand for that kind of workforce is now receding. Deloitte defined future job demand in terms of an 'agile, problem-solving' workforce. This workforce will be occupationally mobile.[73] Portfolio careers will be common. Persons will not stay in one job but will move between jobs. This, in turn, is an expression of a deeper intellectual agility, the capacity to see commonalities in things that are different. This is not a function of intelligence but of imagination.

In 2014, 35 percent of persons in the UK workforce had a degree. In the auto-industrial age, qualifications will matter less not more. Post-industrial mass university education was discipline-focused and template-driven. It was focused on producing large numbers of graduates to undertake routine office-and-sales work. Problem solving, let alone higher forms of creativity, was tacitly ignored or downplayed in most of the post-industrial tertiary curricula which empha-sized the reproduction of text book-style formula knowledge. Likewise, digital know-how was rarely effectively integrated into such curricula. The mass uni-versity used terms like 'digital', 'creativity' and 'innovation' rhetorically. But the post-industrial university displayed little interest in, understanding of or feel for either acts of creation or automation. It saw itself instead as furnishing quali-fied labour for an ever-expanding public sector and corporate domain that was devoted to ever-increasing rule production and regulation.

Periodically after 1970 words like 'inter-disciplinary' or 'trans-disciplinary' came into vogue in the universities. Yet these words had no impact on what the universities actually did. Trans-disciplinary fusions of science, technology, arts and business were in practice alien to the post-industrial academic mind. The drive of universities was to provide mass education. Trans-disciplinary cognition pointed in the opposite direction — away from routinized mass reproduction and replication. In the auto-industrial age, demand for mid-tier qualifications (the bachelor's degree) will decrease. The demand for scarce cross-over abili-ties will rise. Many existing universities will struggle to adapt to this change. Creative fusions of technology, the arts, business and science are not their stock-in-trade. Deloitte today wonders aloud 'are universities teaching the right things?'[74] The answer is: no. They have a deep aversion to melding science, technology, engineering and mathematics with the arts (humanities, social sci-ences and creative arts) and business and law. Yet the dynamic components of advanced economies and societies are fusion-driven.

The most successful corporation of the first decade of the twenty-first cen-tury was Apple. It exemplified a cross-over technology-design-business ethos. In 2015 it was worth more than the entire 1977 US stock market.[75] Successful future businesses arguably will look more like Apple than not. In 2010 the com-pany's founder, Steve Jobs, publicly declared that he saw Apple as 'existing at the intersection of technology and the liberal arts.' He demurred when later asked whether that was really technology, the liberal arts *and* commerce. That demur-ral was less disingenuous than it might appear. It is entirely consistent with the view of supply side economics. From Jean-Baptiste Say onwards, the argument has been that *supply creates demand*. That is to say, if a company supplies inge-nious interesting products, those products will create their own demand. On that view, commerce is a derivative consequence of combining 'technology and the liberal arts'. Yet, ironically, universities (whose members on the whole despise commerce) are consistently unable to coalesce 'technology and the liberal arts'. The liberal arts component of universities has halved since the 1970s. It is dying. The need for inventive combinations of technology and the arts, commerce and science exists. Yet the post-industrial universities have been unable to produce such combinations in ways that work. They cannot put together what stands apart. They cannot do so because, in truth, they are not very creative.

On the whole the post-industrial universities prefer to offer third-rate 'studies' built on low-level intellectual content to students with ever-decreasing entry scores who then graduate to work in service jobs that do not require a university degree. Many graduates today who do better than this, who work in offices, are in jobs that will be computerized. Thirty percent of today's graduate jobs are projected to be replaced by machines.[76] The post-industrial universities are ill-equipped to meet this challenge. This is not least because the demand for mass higher education will decline in step with computerization. In all probability, unforeseen new occupations and new industries will arise in the auto-industrial age. It is, as has been noted, an open question whether the numbers employed in those occupations and industries will match in real terms the numbers who will be disemployed as automation expands. Irrespective, it is clear that demand for university graduates will decline in the auto-industrial era. As it is today demand is already weaker than the supply.

A reduction in demand for graduates does not necessarily mean generalized unemployment. It does though point to a different pattern of employment — more self-employment, more high school graduates going straight into the workforce or into short certificate programs before entering the workforce. There are already signs today that students leaving high school are resisting the social pressure to go to college or university.[77] As auto-industrialism expands, the centrality of universities to the workforce will decline. As it does, there will be pressure on universities to meet the more complex challenge of servicing a smaller high-performance workforce that integrates arts, technology and business — or (on a more abstract level) machines, patterns and persons.

NOTES

1. In his play *R.U.R.* (*Rossum's Universal Robots*), Čapek said of his imaginative creation: they remember everything and think of nothing new. Domin, the factory director character in the play, quipped 'They'd make fine university professors'. Robot was a derivative of Czech word 'robota', a term for drudgery or servitude.

2. The comparatively much larger expenditure on post-war road construction in the United States in the period 1953–73 yielded an estimated 1 percent growth premium.

3. Industrial Robot Statistics: ifr.org.
4. This complements the trend to outsource and relocate white-collar backroom work overseas, a move that can reduce salary costs to a fifth of onshore costs. IT makes possible the relocation of HR, payroll and similar functions to lower-salary countries with a qualified workforce. The eventual automation of such work is a function of economics. Any clerical function ultimately will be automated once the price of automation falls below the price of employing a white-collar workforce offshore.
5. Guest Writer (2014). Chapman (2014) observed: 'For tax and BAS agents, it means that their role as intermediaries between clients and the ATO could be rendered redundant.' The Australian Government calls this Standard Business Reporting (SBR). It promises that in the future 'the majority of business management software will have SBR enabled functionality'. SBR-enabled software transcript: sbr.gov.au.
6. Frey and Osborne (2013).
7. Deloitte (2014).
8. Sui and Jaimovich (2015).
9. Frey and Osborne (2013, section III).
10. Gates (2007: 58–65).
11. 'Accurate biological models of the brain would have to include some 225,000,000,000,000,000 (225 million billion) interactions between cell types, neurotransmitters, neuromodulators, axonal branches and dendritic spines, and that doesn't include the influences of dendritic geometry, or the approximately 1 trillion glial cells which may or may not be important for neural information processing. Because the brain is nonlinear, and because it is so much larger than all current computers, it seems likely that it functions in a completely different fashion ... The brain-computer metaphor obscures this important, though perhaps obvious, difference in raw computational power.' (Chatham, 2007).
12. Deloitte (2014: 10).
13. Deloitte Access Economics (2014).
14. PricewaterhouseCoopers (2001).
15. According to 2008 OECD figures, Australia's healthcare costs were 8.5 percent of GDP, 17.7 percent of government revenue was spent on health, and government covered 67.5 percent of health costs. In the United States, the figures were 16.0 percent of GDP and 18.5 percent of government revenue for government coverage of 45.1 percent of health costs.
16. Frey and Osborne (2015, figures 48, 60).
17. A counterview is offered by Robert Gordon (2016) who says, 'I am looking over the entire economy and I am seeing sector after sector where we're not finding much influence of technology at all. Take the grocery store, we have checking out with bar-code scanning, pretty similar to what we have had for the last twenty or thirty years, with most payment taking place with credit cards instead of cash or cheque ... I play a game called find the robot where I look everywhere in my daily life not just in the supermarket but throughout retail, checking in for a doctors'

appointment, throughout the educational industry which I'm a part of, looking for examples of modern artificial intelligence or robots taking over human jobs and I find that the techno-optimists are just greatly exaggerating the span or sphere of life that will be impacted by these innovations that are indeed gradually happening ... There's opportunity for progress but think of the typical hospital with the kinds of things nurse and orderlies do for patients. There's room for perhaps robots to push patient beds through the hallways to go from a hospital room to get a cat-scan or x-ray and bring the patient back, replacing human labour but we're a long way from having robots that are capable of doing virtually anything that a human nurse is capable of doing much less a doctor.'

18. Reuters (2016) profiles the US Sea Hunter robotic submarine hunting warship. The United States is also developing robot submarines for long-duration intelligence, surveillance and reconnaissance operations. Tomaszewski (2015).

19. The consulting firm McKinsey (2016) expects that 'up to 15 percent of new cars sold in 2030 could be fully autonomous'.

20. Demetriou (2015). Ten human staff only function behind the automated scenes.

21. Borghina (2015); Freyberg (2011).

22. Crawford (2014).

23. The lower prices that accompany automation further encourage consumers to adopt them.

24. Murphy (2015b).

25. Smashing Robotics (2016) lists examples of exoskeleton technology, including Hybrid Assistive Limb, SuitX, Ekso and HULC.

26. Levy (2012).

27. Brynjolfsson and McAfee (2014).

28. This is having political effects. Pre-digital post-industrial media organizations were strongly biased to the political left. Many of these gatekeepers are now out of business or going to be out of business.

29. Frey and Osborne (2013).

30. Acemoglu and Autor (2012: 461).

31. Hicks (2013).

32. Kassamali and Ladak (2015).

33. Wiltz (2013).

34. www.isur.eu/isur/

35. By a MIT, Tokyo Institute of Technology and Sheffield University team. Bodkin (2016).

36. Unassisted diagnosis is incorrect in an estimated 20 percent of cases. Electronic diagnostic assistance has the advantage of computers that can keep up with the 185,000 medical trials that occur each year.

37. Frey and Osborne (2013).

38. The opposite view is summed by Richard Watson (2016): 'A meta-study of thousands of research papers about education, produced by Australian academic John Hattie from the University of Melbourne concluded with a league table of teaching innovations or interventions. Guess what's top of the class in terms of results?

The answer is people. Or more specifically, the interaction between teachers and pupils in a classroom.' One might reasonably wonder though whether this literature is self-serving. Watson suggests that the most important factor in education is not children learning through laissez-faire discovery but teachers building up a bedrock of knowledge through classroom interaction. There is strong reason for thinking though that the converse is true. The autodidactic DIY model of education produced Jane Austen, James Baldwin, Alexander Graham Bell, William Blake, Elizabeth Barrett Browning, Andrew Carnegie, Agatha Christie, Samuel Clemens, Grover Cleveland, Joseph Conrad, Ezra Cornell, Walt Disney, Thomas Edison, Michael Faraday, Henry Ford, Henry George, Charlotte Perkins Gillman, Jane Goodall, Patrick Henry, Soichiro Honda, Elias Howe, Bernard Kerik, William Lear, Doris Lessing, Abraham Lincoln, John Major, Herman Melville, Adolph Ochs, Alexander Pope, Beatrix Potter, Harold Ross, David Sarnoff, Herbert Spencer, Quentin Tarantino, Harry Truman, George Washington, Orville and Wilbur Wright, and Frank Lloyd Wright. See autodidactic.com, Profiles.

39. Mangu-Ward (2013); Epistemic Games (2013).

40. McFarland (2016).

41. Exciting elevating personal interactions in the form of 'great teaching' will continue on as before. That said, 'great teaching' is far less common than sometimes claimed. Nor is it clear that 'teaching' as such is the most effective medium for learning. As one advocate of the DIY home school model (Hennessey, 2016) put it: 'the job of the homeschooling parent is to instill in the homeschooled child a love of learning. In our house, that means a love of books. We've got loads of them. And we can walk to the library to get more if we need them. So long as we have that, there's nothing we can't learn on our own. We also have a computer. You probably do, too. This is 2016. It's the Internet age. You don't need an education degree anymore to locate the resources to educate a child. Everything you need is online.' The scholastic performance of the DIY home-schooled child exceeds that of the institutionally-schooled child; additionally, the parental income of home-schooled children is lower than average. Murphy (2015a: 214).

42. BLS Employment Projections program, Table 1.7 Occupational employment and job openings data, projected 2012–22 and worker characteristics, 2012.

43. US National Centre for Education Statistics, Table 1 Educational attainment of the population 18 years and over, by age, sex, race and Hispanic origin: 2014. For those in the workforce, the figures are: less than high school 8.9 percent; high school diploma or equivalent 24.6 percent; some college 9.3 percent; associate degree 9.3 percent; bachelor's degree 22.1 percent; master's degree 9.4 percent; doctoral or professional degree 4.1 percent. BLS Employment Projections program, Table 1.11 Educational attainment for workers 25 years and older by detailed occupation, 2012-13.

44. US National Centre for Education Statistics, Table 302.60 Percentage of 18- to 24-year-olds enrolled in degree-granting institutions, by level of institution and sex and race/ethnicity of student: 1967 through 2012.

45. In 2010, of 822 BLS-listed US occupations, only in the case of 195 (23 percent) of those occupations did 70 percent or more in the occupation have a bachelor's or higher degree. The most common calls for degree holders were in the following professional fields: finance, mathematics and computing, architecture and engineering, science, counselling, law, teaching, writing, medical and health. BLS Employment Projections program, Table 1.11 Educational attainment for workers 25 years and older by detailed occupation, 2010–11.

46. US higher education numbers: 21,016,126 (2010), 20,994,113 (2011), 20,642,819 (2012), 19,105,651 (2013), 18,948,521 (2014), 18,592,605 (2015). Data sources: US National Center for Education Statistics and US National Student Clearinghouse Research Center.

47. http://music.ucsc.edu/faculty/david-cope

48. Murphy (2012: 82–96).

49. Google N-gram analysis shows that the term was popular between 1750 and 1850, then declined in popularity to 1910, then rose sharply again in the period through to 1928, falling away only to rise again after 1994 during the information society wave.

50. Burnham (2014/1964).

51. Barack Obama's presidency idolized intelligence. The president repeatedly told the story of how his secretary of energy from 2009 to 2013, Steven Chu, was a Nobel Prize winner (1997). The Obama administration by implication was smart. It epitomized cleverness, canniness, brightness and braininess. Reality suggested otherwise, though. A trawl through the statistics on Obama's America revealed a portrait of stagnant real incomes, atrophying wealth, struggling industries and emaciated opportunities. The supposedly quick, sharp and keen administration did practically nothing to kick-start upward mobility, real income increases, rapid GDP growth, or any of the other measures of economic and social prosperity. The kind of American left-liberalism that the administration was rooted in developed early in the twentieth century as an alternative to European socialism. American liberals desired a socially benevolent form of capitalism, one tamed by the state. They acknowledged that capitalism could not be replaced. But they were intent on transforming it internally. The state could not run an economy. That was the delusion of socialism. But the state could regulate capitalism. It could subject it to norms, rules, policies, indicators, measures, standards, laws, reviews, studies, examinations, evaluations, in short 'intelligence'. The resulting long-term economic and social performance though suggested that far from accelerating prosperity and happiness, 'intelligence' stymied it.

52. See, e.g., Dewey (1948 [1920]; 1959 [1929]).

53. The reasons for this are discussed in Murphy (2015a).

54. Murphy (2012: 6–8).

55. 3D printers have been developed to print cookies, ice creams, desserts, chocolates, confections, pastas, pizzas and specialized nursing home preparations among many other food items. The technology permits the creation of foods that are intricately

designed and personalized. Specialist 3D print food shops and outlets are likely to develop. Instead of shopping for prepackaged cookies, consumers could select cookie blueprints from among thousands of possible designs and print them out.

56. Venture capitalists have a rule of thumb for investing in new businesses. They want to know from the budding entrepreneur whether the business will reduce the pain of the consumer — for the larger the pain (or problem), the more the consumer will want the product. 'Everyone thinks his or her startup solves a consumer pain point. However, ask yourself metaphorically if the pain point you solve is "aspirin level" or is it "morphine level?" Big VCs love to invest in businesses that solve morphine-level pain. Why? Because when pain is huge, it's far likelier consumers will pay for the solution. Businesses that solve minor inconveniences usually hit a brick wall when they try and monetize or scale and don't usually get funded.' Gandhi (2015).

57. US National Endowment for the Arts, 2013, ACPSA tables.

58. A similar approach but in a more conventional globalized vein can be observed in the operations of a successful contemporary international clothing retailer like the Australian company Cotton On that sells fashionably designed, modestly priced basics in-store and online. The business employs a large team of designers and trend forecasters. It manufactures its clothing in over 300 factories in China and Bangladesh. The turnaround time between design and manufacture is 2 to 8 weeks. It ships its product to seven distribution centres located in Brisbane, China, California, Singapore, South Africa, Melbourne and New Zealand. Mitchell (2015).

59. Photographic arts, which rose in the mid-nineteenth century, are a classic example of the merger of art and technology in the industrial age. Media arts and digital design follow in the footsteps of this as does recorded music.

60. Mohdin (2015).

61. Key to this in the twentieth century was the linguistic paradigm, the governing metaphor that turned all disciplines into the handmaidens of the discipline of language.

62. Historically, there is an intimate causal link between the aesthetic patterns of great cities and their might, commercial and otherwise. See Murphy (2001).

63. Hofstadter and Sander (2013).

64. Murphy (2012: 53–4, 78–9, 135).

65. Somers (2013).

66. 800–1,200 per day compared with 300–500. Oh (2016); see also Zhou (2015). In Victoria, one of Australia's six states, with a population of 5.7 million, 200,000 bricks are laid each day.

67. More than a decade ago, Virginia Postrel (2003) observed the following: '...entrepreneurial kids from shop class and cosmetology school are doing all right. They're leaving the factories — or never entering them in the first place — and confounding conventional expectations about what it means to be a blue-collar worker or a service provider. For instance, the number of manicurists has tripled in a decade, to nearly 350,000, while the number of nail salons doubled. What's more, stone

fabricators, who turn granite and marble slabs into countertops, are opening thousands of new businesses a year, and sales appear recession-proof. Car customizers now roam the Las Vegas Specialty Equipment Market Association trade show, four times the size of Comdex, checking out the latest in engines, wheels, accessories, and hot, hot cars. Sales grew 46 percent from 1996 to 2001, to about $26 billion. The purely aesthetic part of the market tops $10 billion. The number of graphic designers in the US has grown tenfold in a generation, to an estimated 150,000.' The BLS in 2015 reported that there were 259,500 graphic designers working in the United States, earning a median pay of $44,000 a year and generally possessing a bachelor's degree. Manicurists, estheticians, cosmetologists and hairdressers numbered 793,000 and earned income in the $20,000 range. Mostly these jobs were filled by high school graduates with a postsecondary non-degree award. Automotive body and glass repairers were high school graduates with on-the-job training, earning $38,000 a year.

68. 'First, these companies are essentially product design teams that are focused on iterating fast to find product-market fit. They are able to offer fundamentally better products and services than the incumbents because of the product-centric DNA of the management teams. They usually focus their product development on a sub-segment of the millennial demographic because millennial customers don't have much loyalty to existing brands ... Second, these companies rent all aspects of operational scale from partners and eliminate any capital expenditures or operational inertia from their execution plans. They are therefore designed for growth, especially given their lean organizational structures. For manufacturing, logistics, customer acquisition and commerce, there are third party services and APIs available to scale with customer demand as quickly as necessary.' Taneja (2015).

69. Cowen (2013).

70. Or — to put it another way — what is the relative value of queuing for a quick quip from the counter clerk versus getting your burger-and-fries immediately from the counter robot serving up the food made by the hamburger robot? Would you know the difference, if you sat the Turing taste test, between the human-made burger and the robot-made burger? Will you be able to tell the difference between 3D-printed food in the future and regular food?

71. Murphy (2015a, 2016).

72. Deloitte (2014: 15).

73. Deloitte (2014: 16).

74. Deloitte (2014: 18).

75. Fry (2015).

76. Deloitte (2014: 15).

77. Cavendish (2015).

Table 1 US employment by major occupational group, 2014 and projected to 2024

2014 US National Employment Matrix title and code		Employment, 000s		Change 2014–24, 000s		Median annual wage, 2014[1]	Occupation growth vs. population growth, 2014–24	Percent self-employed, 2014	Percent self-employed, 2014
		2014	2024	Number	Percent				
Total, all occupations	00-0000	150,539.9	160,328.8	9,788.9	6.5	$35,540		6.2%	
Farming, fishing and forestry occupations	45-0000	972.1	914.9	−57.2	−5.9	$20,250		4.6%	
Production occupations	51-0000	9,230.3	8,948.3	−282.1	−3.1	$31,720		2.6%	
Office and administrative support occupations	43-0000	22,766.1	23,232.6	466.5	2.0	$32,520		1.1%	
Architecture and engineering occupations	17-0000	2,532.7	2,599.9	67.2	2.7	$75,780		2.9%	
Arts, design, entertainment, sports and media occupations	27-0000	2,624.2	2,731.7	107.5	4.1	$45,180	Below projected 8% population growth rate	25.3%	5.6%
Protective service occupations	33-0000	3,443.8	3,597.7	153.9	4.5	$37,180		0.5%	
Transportation and material moving occupations	53-0000	9,748.5	10,215.3	466.8	4.8	$29,530		3.8%	
Sales and related occupations	41-0000	15,423.1	16,201.1	778.0	5.0	$25,360		7.6%	
Legal occupations	23-0000	1,268.2	1,332.8	64.6	5.1	$76,860		15.4%	
Management occupations	11-0000	9,157.5	9,662.9	505.4	5.5	$97,230		20.3%	
Building and grounds cleaning and maintenance occupations	37-0000	5,617.2	5,967.0	349.8	6.2	$23,270		12.4%	

(Continued)

Table 1 (Continued)

2014 US National Employment Matrix title and code		Employment, 000s		Change 2014–24, 000s		Median annual wage, 2014[1]	Occupation growth vs. population growth, 2014–24	Percent self-employed, 2014	Percent self-employed, 2014
		2014	2024	Number	Percent				
Installation, maintenance and repair occupations	49-0000	5,680.5	6,046.0	365.5	6.4	$42,110		5.0%	
Food preparation and serving related occupations	35-0000	12,467.6	13,280.4	812.9	6.5	$19,130		0.6%	
Life, physical and social science occupations	19-0000	1,310.4	1,408.0	97.6	7.4	$61,450		5.8%	
Education, training and library occupations	25-0000	9,216.1	9,913.7	697.6	7.6	$46,660		2.1%	
Business and financial operations occupations	13-0000	7,565.3	8,197.8	632.4	8.4	$64,790		5.4%	
Construction and extraction occupations	47-0000	6,501.7	7,160.7	659.0	10.1	$41,380	Above projected 8% population growth rate	17.4%	
Community and social service occupations	21-0000	2,465.7	2,723.4	257.7	10.5	$41,290		2.1%	
Computer and mathematical occupations	15-0000	4,068.3	4,599.7	531.4	13.1	$79,420		2.6%	
Personal care and service occupations	39-0000	6,006.1	6,798.2	792.1	13.2	$21,260		17.1%	8.6%
Healthcare practitioners and technical occupations	29-0000	8,236.5	9,584.6	1,348.1	16.4	$61,710		2.9%	
Healthcare support occupations	31-0000	4,238.0	5,212.2	974.2	23.0	$26,440		3.5%	

Data source: BLS Employment Projections program, Table 1.1 Employment by major occupational group, 2014 and projected 2024; Table 1.7 Occupational employment and job openings data, projected 2014–24, and worker characteristics, 2014.

Source: Employment Projections program, U.S. Department of Labor, U.S. Bureau of Labor Statistics

1 Data are from the Occupational Employment Statistics program, U.S. Department of Labor, U.S. Bureau of Labor Statistics.

2

INDUSTRY

RISE AND FALL

Industrial growth eventually means industrial decline. It happens to all industries in every industrial society. No matter how much they might expand, eventually they will shrink. Their seeming implacable dominance is but a prelude to their eventual demotion and relegation. Most people in the nineteenth century in the major economies earned their livelihood from agriculture. Today hardly anyone does.[1] Generally speaking now the more advanced an economy is the greater the portion of employment and output devoted to services. Services is a motley category. It incorporates retail and wholesale occupations, utilities, transport and warehousing, information, financial, professional and business services, education and health, leisure and hospitality and government. In 1970, 30 percent of Americans worked in secondary industry; in 2010, 13 percent did.[2] Employment in manufacturing in particular shrank. In 1970, 25 percent of Americans worked in manufacturing; in 2010, only 10 percent did. In 2000, 17.3 million were employed in US manufacturing; by 2016, the number had fallen to 12.3 million.[3] In Australia in the decade through to 2013–14, employment in manufacturing declined by 92,000 jobs while jobs in health-care and social services grew by 462,000, professional services by 314,000 and construction by 220,000.[4]

The shrinkage of manufacturing is often attributed to globalization: the relocation of manufacturing plants from high-wage to low-wage countries. An alternate explanation is 'unfair competition' from mercantilist states. These states subsidize manufacturing or else protect the sector with tariffs. But in reality a far deeper process than either mercantilism or globalization is at work. The longer term trend is for manufacturing *everywhere* to shrink even in countries with cheap labour. Manufacturing's share of employment peaked in Brazil in

1986, in India in 2002 and in China in the mid-1990s.[5] The share of national employment though should not be confused with manufacturing's productive capacity. Even after the rise of China as a manufacturing giant, the United States remained the world's number two manufacturer, trending only slightly behind China in output. In fact, US manufacturing's long-term output share of American real GDP remained constant between 1960 and 2010, at around 12 percent.[6] In effect the sector's contribution to wealth creation remained steady over time while its share of employment declined markedly.

As manufacturing employment has fallen, the service sector's share of employment has risen. In the United States, it soared from 64 percent of jobs in 1970 to 84 percent in 2010.[7] This trend is reflected worldwide. In 1980, services accounted for 50 percent of global output. Today the figure is 70 percent.[8] Seventy-one percent of Brazil's GDP, 52 percent of India's and 48 percent of China's are made up of services.[9] The future then is services. Or is it? 'We are moving towards a knowledge and service economy'.[10] That was true of the post-industrial age after 1970. For mid-tier global economies, like China, it remains true for the mid-range future. Yet whether it is true of the most advanced economies today is another matter. For these are already service economies. Today services in the United Kingdom are 78 percent of GDP; the United States 78 percent; France 78 percent; Belgium 77 percent; Denmark 76 percent; Singapore 75 percent; Japan 72 percent; Switzerland 73 percent; Sweden 72 percent; Australia 70 percent and Germany 69 percent.[11] Hong Kong sits at the pinnacle. Ninety-two percent of its economic output is in services.

In modern economies what rises falls. The motion of the modern industrial economy is not linear. Rather it follows a cyclical 'growth-and-shrinkage' pattern. This undulating pattern swells and surges but then recedes. The holy grail of a modern industrial economy is productivity. Productivity means producing more with less: more output utilizing less labour. This is achieved by labour substitution, in the short run by replacing expensive with cheaper labour; in the longer run by replacing labour with machines. This happened in primary industries. It has happened in secondary industries. In the tertiary or services sector, it has not yet happened. But it will happen. There are already signs that auto-industrialism will eventually bring major productivity gains to the services sector. This means that the demand for service sector employees will decline.

Once services reach their peak, as secondary industries did in the leading economies in the 1960s, the service sector share of employment will diminish. Sector growth and shrinkage is a long-term process. It takes decades to unfold. But unfold it does, inexorably. Nobody decrees the underlying undulating process. The waves of industrialization and deindustrialization, job expansion and automation, are not authorized or designed by anyone. They are just an inherent feature of industrial economies. Policies and laws may delay or speed up the process a smidgeon. But no policy, law or regulation, and no incentive scheme or national plan, can reverse or obstruct the wave-like motion that lies at the heart of industrial economies.

INDUSTRY DEVELOPMENT

Automation sheds labour. We saw this in the nineteenth century in agriculture and in the twentieth century in manufacturing. In the twenty-first century, automation will reduce employment in the tertiary industries. Gradually work in the office, sales and service sector will be replaced by machines. Given that, let us try a thought experiment. Suppose that automation continues incrementally and relentlessly across primary, secondary and tertiary industries. But that mass unemployment does not follow. This means that either some segments of existing industries will manage to doggedly resist automation or else a new quaternary layer of industries will fill the gap that has been left by the industries that need fewer and fewer employees.[12]

In the short term some existing industries will maintain and in some cases even increase their labour share. In the longer run, even these hold-outs will decline in size and number. The future has two temporal horizons. There is the near-run future, the next decade. This is a function of present trends combined with incipient transformations. There is also the longer-term future when the fuller effect of auto-industrialism will be felt. The large-scale shift in the pattern of industries is liable to take 40 to 60 years to fully unfold. To put this in context: the post-industrial era dominated by sales, office and service work ran from 1970 to 2010. The near future will see a disruption of that model. The longer-term future will see the eventual demise of post-industrialism and the rise of quaternary industries.

INDUSTRY IN THE NEAR FUTURE

The US BLS provides 10-year labour force projections.[13] These projections are just that — projections. They are fallible. We cannot over-rely on them. Even in the short run, rapid technology changes can undermine them. That said a number of trends are evident today. The BLS projects that between 2014 and 2024 the American workforce will grow 6.5 percent.[14] This compares with a projected population growth of 8 percent over the same period.[15] A few areas only of likely employment increase matches or exceeds expected population growth. The strongest areas of labour force growth today are in the *calculation-construction-and-care* segments of the economy.

Paralleling this, the post-industrial office-and-sales workforce is visibly losing momentum. BLS data estimates for high and low growth occupational categories for the near future are instructive. Table One depicts clearly the contraction of employment in primary, secondary and tertiary sectors. The post-industrial era is winding down. This applies at both ends of the post-industrial spectrum. Service, office and sales work is decelerating as are higher-end legal, management and education occupations. High-growth occupations in the near future fall into three clusters: *the calculation cluster* (business and financial operations; computing and mathematical analysis), *the care cluster* (personal care and healthcare) and *the construction cluster*.

The expansion of healthcare is a function of an aging population. The number of Americans aged 65 years and older will rise from 15 percent of the population in 2015 to 19 percent in 2025, and then less sharply to 21 percent in 2035 after which the percentage will plateau through to 2055. Of all the near-term, high-growth occupations, the one that is the most problematic in the longer term is the fastest growing in the short term, i.e. healthcare. This paradox results from the fact that healthcare today is a highly institutionalized low productivity industry.[16] In the past three decades health costs in advanced economies have increased well in excess of inflation, population growth and the population aging factor. Government regulation and broader post-industrial bureaucratization have contributed significantly to this. At the same time escalating investments in health research and development have yielded diminishing returns.[17] Health systems are ripe for the auto-industrialization of administration and many routine delivery functions. One of the likely benefits of the long-run auto-industrialization of the health industry will be to reduce the institutional factor in healthcare and increase the personal independence factor. Quaternary industries have a high autonomy component; tertiary industries have a low autonomy component.

The near-term growth of the calculation employment cluster in part reflects the historic shift of national income in the major economies from wage and salary-based income to capital-based income. Capital work has a higher calculation component. The growth in importance of calculation also reflects more generally the central role that numbers play in technological, scientific, economic, political and social matters. Calculation is critical to unravelling the abstract patterns of nature and society. Markets, industries, cities and publics are governed by abstract dynamics. Numbers are essential to social actors being able to effectively understand these dynamics and adapt to them. Calculation is often more effective in guaranteeing human autonomy in the face of social abstraction than is either legislation or regulation. Autonomy has a number of social expressions. One of its expressions is individuals figuring out how to fit comfortably into larger-scale anonymous social generalities. Calculation mediates between autonomy and abstraction.

Another essential expression of human autonomy is non-institutional identities. Both the mass-industrial and post-industrial eras were strongly institutional in nature. Big organizations dominated both. Auto-industrialism promises disintermediation and a significant degree of deinstitutionalization. The appetite for a disintermediated world is reflected in the spirited near-term growth of the personal care and construction industries — or at least key components of these industries. The quaternary autonomy impulse is quietly echoed in the substantial growth in the size and aesthetic sophistication of personal dwellings and also in spending on personal appearance, travel guides, recreation and fitness, and personal aides. In part these are services; in part not. A service is something that a person receives. When an ISP, for example, provides a service, the customer does little more than pay for it. Services of this kind are prone to automation. In quaternary industries customers are more active or involved. They do not just passively buy or receive a good. They also actively invest time, energy and emotion alongside that of the producer or the service provider. The house buyer today is much more likely to be a home improver than the house purchaser of 70 years ago. In a disintermediated world, a media company provides streaming services and the consumer makes their own scheduling and programming choices. This is sharply different from the tertiary service model of the television network broadcaster.

Economic actors in the quaternary sector behave differently from those in the service command economy. The latter was the product of the organizational age that began in earnest in the 1920s. The growth today of a quaternary layer of disintermediated products and DIY services and activities does not mean the extinction of primary, secondary or tertiary industries. These will continue on. Their productivity will increase while their labour force in real terms will decline. This means that the pattern of occupational growth and shrinkage is different from the pattern of industry revenue growth and shrinkage. An industry can grow in revenue or profitability or output yet shrink in share of employment. Income from capital and labour are not locked in a fixed ratio or relationship. If we consider the 2010–16 period for example, fast-growing US businesses were predominately in the transport and automotive, creative, calculation, care and construction industry segments.[18] Yet it was only in the case of the latter three (calculation, care and construction) were there serious expectations of significant employment growth in the decade to follow (see Table 1).[19]

This is a reflection of the long-term law of industrialization. In time, machines will replace labour in all industries. The post-industrial creative industries are an example of this. In the United States in the period 2014–24, jobs in those industries are expected to grow at a rate of only about half of the rate of population growth. This reflects significant industry disintermediation. Television networks are being replaced by streaming services and newspapers by Internet sites. The creative industries are going the way of the earlier classic production industries like the automotive industry where labour was replaced by machines. Fewer jobs though does not necessarily mean less wealth or productive output. The creative industries are just as likely to generate royalty income (from intellectual property) as to generate employee wage or salary income. Consequently this is an industry sector whose outlook is mixed. In the near term it will employ a decreasing number of persons relative to population while expanding the automated disintermediated digital distribution of creative artefacts that attract license fees.

While it is true that many of the most demanding or difficult kinds of non-routine work are creative in nature, one should not confuse this with the idea that the jobs of the future will be in the creative industries. It is arguable in a loose sense that the social demand for creative labour is increasing. Analysts from the libertarian right, the political centre and the liberal left are in agreement on this point. Tyler Cowen, Erik Brynjolfsson and Andrew McAfee, and Thomas L. Friedman and Michael Mandelbaum all say the same thing.[20] Yet while future work may demand increased degrees of problem solving, adaptability, resourcefulness and imagination, it is important to analytically distinguish between creative work and creative capital. Much of the economic value in the creative industries derives not from salaried employment but rather from the intellectual capital that is represented by designs, compositions and patterns. On top of this, the more regular kind of capital (machine capital) plays an ever-growing role in the distribution of creative artefacts.

This interplay of machine capital, intellectual capital and labour is not peculiar to the creative industries. A classic manufacturing industry like the vehicle and auto parts industry exhibits a similar mix. Aesthetic and performance design is a crucial factor in vehicle sales. In the United States, the vehicle and auto parts industry has been replacing factory labour with machines since the 1960s. In 1990 the industry had 1,054,400 employees (0.8 percent of the total workforce); in 2015, 910,000 employees (0.6 percent of the total workforce).[21] In both years, 1990 and 2015, the United States produced around 12 million vehicles. A mix of machines, labour and industrial aesthetics was a common feature of production in both the mass-industrial and post-industrial eras. The weight of these different elements changed over time but the mix was enduring. The auto-industrial age promises to add to this mix the factor of disintermediation. One can foresee a time in the not-too-distant future when a purchaser of a vehicle will not venture to a showroom to test-drive or pick up a new car. A self-driving car will drive itself to the customer's home. Vehicle purchases will be carried out online. Car distribution thereby will be disintermediated. In mass-industrial and post-industrial eras the machine and the aesthetic capital component of the industry grew. The labour component declined. This will continue in the future. Labour will gravitate to disintermediated businesses. It will swap wage-work for capital-work. Automation in secondary and tertiary industries will be matched by the production of autonomy in the quaternary industries.

INDUSTRY IN THE LONGER TERM

By 2025, in a decade's time, technologies that presently are experimental will begin to appear commonplace. The personal computer was the tool of hobbyists and early adopters in the mid-1980s. A decade later it had become a mass consumer item. In the same way by the mid-2020s, driverless transport vehicles and fully automated peopleless warehouses will have begun to transform the distribution service industry. So, assuming that no unemployment Armageddon follows from this and a quarter of the population is not living on minimum income benefits, what kinds of quaternary industries might we expect to emerge as employment in the older established primary, secondary and tertiary industries continues to decline?

CROSS-OVER INDUSTRIES

Over time in older industries aesthetic and machine capital will continue to grow in importance. Labour will fade in significance. Income generation and distribution will reflect this. The interaction of machine and aesthetic capital will intensify. Take the example of the construction industry. Construction is not an artistic field. Plumbers and tilers are not designers. Nonetheless construction is underpinned by design. The economic and social demand for building is not just for shelter. It is also driven by powerful, demotic aesthetic desires. Both in modern and pre-modern societies, the principal investment in aesthetics that most societies make is what is spent on domestic, commercial and civic building. Function plays its part in every building but function is also overdetermined by form, especially in the most advanced economies. The US BLS projections suggest that, over the foreseeable short term, demand for stonemasons, carpenters, floor layers, tile installers, glaziers, painters and paperhangers will grow. This in its turn points to an important paradox: to be economically sound, growth in employment in a sector has to be matched by the shrinking of employment. Unless this happens, employment growth will result in static or declining efficiencies rather than expanding productivity, the key to long-term economic vibrancy.

The mid-term future of the construction industry hints at both growing job demand combined with a technologically driven reduction in jobs. It is clear that key parts of the building trades will be automated. 3D printing of buildings, the manufacture of buildings in factories, and on-site automated construction (such as the robotic laying of bricks) are some of the techniques that foresee-ably will transform construction techniques, labour demand and productivity. That though is just as liable to be offset by the long-term increasing demand for gilded built space. In the past hundred years, the size of American dwell-ings per capita has doubled in size (from 400 to 800 square feet, or 37 square metres to 74 square metres).[22] House preferences have grown more lavish. The aesthetic and design component of dwellings has expanded. In short, technol-ogy and productivity reduce the need for labour while human desire increases the need for labour.

The affordability of such desires represents the equilibrium point between the pull and push of these contrary economic forces. Technology automates routine work just as demand for non-routine, customized, ornamental or dextrous work increases over time. The occupations that will prosper in the foreseeable future are those built around tasks that cannot be reduced to an algorithm. Many of these will require no more than high school and often less-than-high-school qualifications. In the near term, 50 percent of high-growth occupations will require only high school diplomas or less.[23] These range from orderlies and occupational therapy aides through pest control-lers and baggage porters to fence erectors and segmental pavers to janitors, cleaners, tilers and plasterers.

What about at the high end of the job market? Post-industrial occupa-tions of this kind have been typically defined in terms of field or speciality. This reflected a prevailing analytical way of thinking about occupations. But as we enter the auto-industrial age there are some tell-tale signs that analytical job definitions are starting to break down, at least in the most sought-after occupa-tions. The consultancy firm Deloitte usefully defines such occupations as ones that combine technical, creative and social skills.[24] This echoes the combination of machine capital, aesthetic capital and labour. Many in-demand high-end occupations are transdisciplinary in nature. They integrate aspects of science and technology, art and design, and business and management. That is to say, these are occupations that involve the seamless deployment of machines, patterns and people. They are structurally 'creative' in the sense that they combine professional activities that conventionally tend to be separated. This is also the source of their scarcity. They require cognitive cross-overs that are unusual. Such cross-overs are likely to become more common in high-end occupations in the future.

Thus for example, technology know-how will continue to be in demand. But not necessarily in a stand-alone capacity. At the high point of the post-industrial age, from 1990 to 1999, the demand for IT specialists boomed. Then the IT bubble burst in 2000. Today the demand for information technologists flourishes but less in traditional narrowly defined IT roles and more in hybrid technology-design-business roles. That itself is a microcosm of a larger redefinition of high-demand professions away from the mid-twentieth-century model of the discrete profession defined by a single discipline in the direction of more generalist professional roles incorporating overlapping multi-discipline capacities. The need for professionals to translate and function between the domains of science-technology, humanities-art-design and business-strategic-social science has grown. This reflects a need to combine the understanding of machine operation with pattern formation and people organization. This does not mean the disappearance of the professional discipline specialist. It does mean a growth in demand for transdisciplinary professionals and a shortage of supply of them.

THE AUTONOMOUS ECONOMY

The history of industrial societies suggests that as economic sectors decline new industry sectors emerge. Technology optimists argue that over the long run many more jobs have been created than have been destroyed by machines.[25] Broadly that is true of the industrial age. But is it true of the period since 1990, the second (mature) phase of the post-industrial era, a phase already marked by nascent and incremental auto-industrialization? The Deloitte economist Ian Stewart calculated that since 1992 in the United Kingdom, technology change has caused a two-fold shift: lower-skilled routine occupations have been replaced by higher-skilled non-routine occupations and the number of persons employed has grown from 24.7 million in 1992 to 30.5 million in 2014, a 23 percent positive change. On the surface this figure sounds impressive yet less so when we consider that the UK population over the same period grew 15 percent from 57 million to 64 million. Furthermore, the larger portion of the modest net real occupation growth that did occur over the period was principally in the public sector, that is in teaching, social work, nursing and care work.[26] The prime driver of public sector occupation growth was not technology but rather public spending. UK public spending over the time period grew from 38 percent of GDP to 43 percent of GDP.

Industrial economies grow wealth by increasing productivity. They do this by reducing jobs and replacing them with machines. The mass manufacturing economy has been automated. The post-industrial economy is being automated. The net employment in a society grows when new industry sectors appear. The industrialization of agriculture was offset by the expansion of manufacturing. Then as machines displaced labour in manufacturing, post-industrial office, sales and service jobs grew. Now machines are beginning to replace these jobs.

That begs the question then: what new post-post-industrial sector will arise? Sector substitutes are difficult to identify just as the future is difficult to predict. If auto-industrialism over the long term bites deeply into the tertiary economy, what then will constitute the succeeding quaternary economy? What happens if the numbers of people employed in services in the economic powerhouse nations begin to shrink from 60 or 70 percent of the workforce to 50 or 60 percent? What if the office, sales and service jobs decline by half or more as American manufacturing jobs did over a period of 40 years? What is the substitute for the shrinking post-industrial sector? What in a positive sense does an auto-industrial economy look like? If millions of white-collar and pink-collar jobs in government and hospitality are eventually automated; if transport and warehousing are robotized; if education and health along with professional and business services are auto-industrialized, what kind of post-service outputs and occupations emerge in their stead? What does an auto-industrial economy produce?

Human beings are not going to be content with a neo-patrimonial minimum income economy in which some people work and others receive transfer payments. The transition from a tertiary to a quaternary economy will occur as demand for new types of economic value expands. Such quaternary value entails distinct kinds of satisfactions and gratifications. Agriculture feeds us. Secondary industry produces tangible durable goods. Service industries move, store and sell physical goods, move people and produce intangible goods. The latter include information and advice, entertainment and experience, regulation and gatekeeping industries. A quaternary economy in contrast is a DIY economy. It supports human autonomy. Rather than provide services for persons, it enables human beings to do things for themselves.

Thus for example rather than provide the service of higher education it enables auto-didactic higher education by furnishing an infrastructure of educational materials and competency-based examinations. In the DIY economy, the emphasis is not on receiving goods (be they physical or intangible, artefactual or experiential) but on creating or participating in goods.[27] This is the world of the prosumer rather than the consumer.[28] This is not a world of autarchic personalities insulated from others. In the quaternary economy, as in any other economy, people interact, cooperate and exchange with others. The emphasis though is not on doing something for others (e.g. reporting the news for them) but on enabling them to do it for themselves (by posting online their video of today's natural disaster).

In the quaternary economy, my accountant does not spend much time performing routine services like preparing my tax return (most of that is automated). Rather in a quaternary setting, I have some rough financial plans. The accountant helps me refine and finesse those plans. The key to this process is that it involves a significant DIY component. The emphasis is as much on participation and creation as it is on consumption. I am not just the client or customer but also the co-producer of things, in this case a financial plan. The professional or expert contributes knowledge; the prosumer contributes goals and parameters.

Cisco Systems Internet Business Solutions Group estimates that as of 2006 there were about 14 million prosumers in the United States or about 4.5 percent of the population.[29] The Cisco report concludes that, as a group, prosumers had the following characteristics: a majority (55 percent of them) do some of their work at home, they are higher than average users of laptops, mobile phones and email, they are early adopters of technology, they value being accessible and connected, they are family orientated, they work while commuting, and they are large consumers of media. Seven percent of them are full-time home workers while 11 percent of them run a business from their home. They are a key group among the 60 million Americans who work from home.[30] They are one of the fulfilments of Alvin Toffler's prediction of the rise of the electronic cottage worker.[31]

The prosumer has entered the culture's imaginary. Prosumer television programs like the UK DIY design-and-build-your-own-home program *Grand Designs* are popular. Prosumption has quietly embedded itself in advanced economies. Its varied forms range from user-produced content on media platforms such as YouTube and Instagram to consumers who produce their own electricity and feed the excess power back into the power grid. Self-education has had a major boost from the Internet's almost infinite resources, most recently from the development of open courseware.[32] Prosumer markets for products ranging from cameras to latte makers have emerged. These sell equipment that crosses over between the low end of the professional market and the high end of the consumer market.[33] Companies have surfaced to deliver hospital-standard nursing care to the home market and bulk or wholesale goods into retail precincts.

These developments are classic of acts of creation: they meld antitheses. Just as Toffler's prosumer coinage did in its time. Prosumers are natural auto-industrialists. They want to be involved in some way in the process of producing, distributing or marketing the goods and services that they use or consume. The success of warehouse-style home improvement retailers like America's Home Depot (founded in 1978) or Australia's Bunnings (its superstore format started in 1994) is an indicator of the growth of the prosumer market.[34] Online retail investor services such as company webcasts and email updates, electronic share trading and share registration support the 55 percent of US households and the 20 percent of UK households that own stocks.[35] Premium media services for users who wish to post or blog on broadcast sites are increasingly commonplace.

Prosumers are part of the larger quaternary economy. This is a sector that corrals self-directed forms of economic and industrial activity. It subsumes autonomous technologies, DIY services and platform providers. How large is the quaternary counterpart of primary, secondary and tertiary industries? Taking the US economy, the most sophisticated of all contemporary economies, as the example, roughly estimated the quaternary economy today makes up at least 3 percent of America's $17,000 billion GDP. This compares with American agricultures' 1.4 percent share of GDP. The autonomous economy includes disparate components ranging from the home improvement products market ($313 billion in 2014),[36] the nursery and garden industry ($40 billion in 2015),[37] the bed-and-breakfast industry ($20 billion), social media (in February 2016 the Facebook, LinkedIn and Twitter platforms had a combined 2015 revenue of $22 billion),[38] home schooling ($1 billion in 2010),[39] independent label music production ($366 million),[40] self-publishing (458,564 titles in 2013; $300 million in value),[41] and crafts (including knitting, sewing, quilting $30 billion).[42] The propensity for above-average revenue growth is notable in the quaternary sector. In the period 2010–15, in an otherwise sluggish American economy, with overall growth pegged at 2.2 percent, the bed-and-breakfast industry ($2 billion revenue) grew 4.6 percent p.a.; robotic surgery equipment manufacturing ($2 billion revenue) 10.2 percent p.a. and home improvement stores ($156 billion revenue) 3.8 percent per annum.[43]

The autonomous economy includes large, medium and small businesses. Its defining feature is its yeoman spirit. Its end-point is autonomous DIY independent activities. These are activities animated by a self-determining, self-directed or self-reliant ethos. This is not to be confused with solipsistic, autarchic, or narcissistic behaviours. The self-determining spirit of the modern yeoman enterprise has deep roots. In the United States, its prehistory lies in the Jefferson and Jacksonian eras. These periods mixed the inquiring impulse of the European Enlightenment with the practical exigencies of a then mainly rural American society. Thomas Jefferson notably was an accomplished technologist and inventor, as was Benjamin Franklin.

The rural America that produced the Wright Brothers is long gone. But its experimental DIY impulses translated to urban settings. The turn-of-the-twentieth-century San Francisco Bay Area is a good example. Amateur technology clubs flourished there. Encouraged by Stanford University's engineering department they encouraged interest in and the development of wireless radio technology. A similar thing happened in the 1970s. Amateurs excited by electronics played a decisive role in the development of Silicon Valley's personal computer industry. The early twentieth-century amateur technology movement had a loose parallel in the Arts and Crafts Movement of the period and Gustav Stickley's influential Craftsman style of architecture, furniture and decoration, a meeting point of aesthetics, handicraft and industrial manufacture. The personal computing industry reiterated the cross-over of art and technology when Apple Corp's founder Steve Jobs fused computer technology with mass manufacture and minimalist Modernist industrial aesthetics. Jobs then completed the circle of history when he merged personal computing and wireless technology in the mobile phone.

In any event the quaternary autonomy economy is not new. It has deep historical roots and has demonstrated long-term incremental growth.[44] Over time some autonomous industries (e.g. DIY electronics) have declined. Others have grown. Specialist consumer electronics stores in the United States ($76 billion in revenue employing 326,000 persons) 'grew' 0.7 percent between 2011 and 2016.[45] Amateur electronics by the 2000s had lost the 'radio shack' sheen that it once had in the 1970s and 1980s. Yet it is notable that it was also the seedbed of the mass personal computer manufacturing and service industry that eventually eclipsed it. What this suggests is that the quaternary economy as well as its own productive capacity functions is a breeding ground for more routinized versions of itself which get eventually assimilated into the increasingly automated service and manufacturing economy.

The quaternary economy is not a romanticized antithesis of the routinized economy. Rather it repurposes and remodels materials and artefacts from the routinized economy. The prosumer component of the autonomous economy draws on mass-produced components and equipment like personal computers and mobile phones to self-produce customized artefacts or deliver co-created services. The co-creation and individual customization of value is a hybridization of mass production and tailored production. It merges the traits of the professional and the amateur, mass and bespoke production, into a sinuous 'proateur' synthesis.

THE MAKER MOVEMENT

The merging of mass and tailored production does not signal a nostalgic return to the economy of the pre-industrial craftsman. Nevertheless the quaternary sector, due its emphasis on DIY, at times involves a significant amount of tool use. These are sometimes digital tools, sometimes physical tools. Romantic critics bemoan the loss of the hand tool–using artefact creator. In doing so they overlook the extent to which tool use for artefact production continues to flourish in high-tech settings. That said the more general criticism directed at the post-industrial knowledge economy is valid. The decline of durable object making in the post-industrial world of the office was pronounced. Documents are not durable objects. They are not reusable like furniture or a book is through a long life. The quaternary economy draws its animating spirit in part from the persistence of the human desire to 'objectivate'.[46] This is the in-built desire of human beings to create the kind of lasting objects that constitute humanity's 'second nature'. This is the artificial environment populated by buildings, tools and machines that distinguishes the human world from that of the animal kingdom.

A good example of the contemporary quaternary economy is the makers' movement. In his 2012 book *Makers,* Chris Anderson predicted the coming of a new industrial revolution.[47] This one is based on digital manufacturing methods. These methods are principally of two types. One is computer-aided manufacturing using laser-cutting techniques and robotic devices such as computer numerical control machines. This style of manufacturing is subtractive. It cuts things (such as furniture) out of plastic, wood, metal and other materials. The second type is additive manufacturing or 3D printing.

The desktop factory is just around the corner. Today consumers can buy a 3D printer for $1,000. Soon these will cost $100. 3D printing allows almost anyone to print out almost any object they have designed or else scanned into their design software. I can scan my head and print it out. The same can be done to a screw, a tube, a doorknob, a building, a statue; really anything that can be additively manufactured, which is to say can be printed out by a machine, much like an old-time inkjet printer, that ejects layer upon micro-thin layer of resin or other material and additively builds up the physical object. Soon dentists will routinely print out dental crowns on the spot. Such office-based desktop manufacturing will mean waiting for only an hour for the crown instead of 2 weeks while your dental impression is sent away to a specialist lab to be fabricated. This is practical disintermediation at work.

Houses can be printed out; also foodstuffs, apartment buildings and cars. Ultimately most things can and probably will be printed: from human organs to flutes. Or if not printed, then laser cut. The most interesting aspect of this is how much it will transform the nature of economics. Much that we already know about economies will remain unchanged. Yet some things, and perhaps many things, will change. Modern economies are a function of industrial technology. A powerful new industrial technology is on the horizon. It will not change the basic economics of mass manufacturing. It will still be more economical to mass produce hundreds of thousands of plastic containers using conventional manu-facturing methods. These will still be sourced from China or Bangladesh — or whatever country this year has begun industrialization. As Anderson says, if you want to produce a million rubber ducks, the best way to do that is to invest a lot of money in tooling classic injection-moulding machines. The first duck you produce will cost you $10,000; for every duck after that, the cost reduces. That does not apply to print manufacture. The last 3D print duck you produce will cost you as much as the first one did.

That said, print manufacturing shows signs of developing, potentially on an extensive scale, the custom or boutique production of unique, rare, distinc-tive, personalized, limited-run, tailored, customized or exclusive objects. This is the point at which, conceptually, the prototyping and the production of objects merges into one. Such print-on-demand objects are design-intensive in the traditional nineteenth-century art sense of being 'original'. They are high-technology design-focused artefacts. Computer-aided manufacturing is well suited to such boutique 'protoduction'. Design-driven, low-volume, short-run products are economic to additively manufacture. The print production process is highly adaptable to a state of constantly changing product design, or what is often called rapid prototyping. A digital machine simply prints or cuts out whatever x,y,z coordinates the computer tells it to. No retooling is required. As Anderson notes, variety, complexity and flexibility are virtually costless in digital manufacturing. This makes production geared to rapidly changing designs or unique patterns economical and easy.

Desktop manufacturing will not change the economics of producing millions of the same item. Robotic manufacturing is doing that. The peopleless factory will change the geography and geodynamics of mass manufacturing. It will reverse the trend to globalization. In the past 40 years big manufacturing countries exported their factories overseas. The driver of this was cheaper labour costs. High-tech robotic factories are beginning to alter this dynamic. As robotic manufacture progressively removes labour from the factory process, labour costs become less important and transport costs (location) becomes relatively more important. Distant locations with cheap labour start to be less attractive compared to local sites with lower logistics costs. Already we are seeing a return of factories to the United States. This does not mean the return of production jobs. These will continue to decline as a proportion of the total workforce. The end of the age of globalization is coming. This will affect the geography of wealth creation. If in net terms today 2 percent of an iPhone's price returns to China's low-margin mass manufacturers, in the future that income will decline as robot factories relocate closer to the consumer markets in North America.

China's rulers understand this. They are trying to hasten the transition of China from a manufacturing to a service economy. They are also rapidly robotizing their own factories. 24/7 peopleless factories in Texas and Kansas will compete successfully for high-volume tiny-margin business because they are closer to the end-market. As the labour component declines, the costs of transport, land, taxes and energy become key to manufacturing economics. Nothing though will grow jobs in manufacturing either in the United States or China.

Robots are one side of the equation transforming economies as they move from the post-industrial to the auto-industrial era. Robotic manufacturing represents production on a mass scale. Technology at the same time is enabling production on a mass boutique scale. Objects created at home or in a local 3D print shop or else by a local small-batch boutique producer — all of these also reverse the globalization process but in another way. 3D print production combines computer design files with a printer that prints out the object that the operator or a third party has designed. Design files can be imported online by a producer, a consumer or a retailer from any location across the globe. But the objects themselves will not be imported. They will be printed locally. This will transform international value chains. All of the post-industrial talk about globalization will come to an end in the foreseeable future. Capital (money capital, machine capital, intellectual capital) will continue to move across international borders. But the conventional trade in goods will decline. Relative to the size of the world's population and its wealth, fewer objects will sail half way round the world from a distant factory through multiple hands to the consumer's home.

Trade will be disintermediated. The number of local robotic factories will increase. Weightless 3D designs, a few electronic bytes, will increase in circulation. Banking capital, as ever, will chase businesses — wherever they are. Since the time of Adam Smith and David Ricardo, the assumption has been that, even despite transport costs, a physical object will find a buyer thousands of miles away because it can be manufactured cheaper or better far away from home. That is all that globalization is — or was. Some of that will remain and some of it will disappear. Automated mass manufacturing relying on robots will produce few new jobs except for a small number of high-skill, high-wage technicians and employees. Already today traditional big businesses are not the prime job creators. Job creation is concentrated among small and medium enterprises. This is where a disintermediated capitalism comes into its own.

Anderson observes that 3D and computer-aided manufacturing combines digital bits and physical atoms.[48] It merges virtual computer-aided design with the production of objects. The merging of the virtual and the physical gives this technology real bite. It will not replace mass manufacturing. 3D printing, as noted, does not offer classic economies of scale. Print technology, however, offers the prospect of large markets emerging for the sale of niche products. Mass customization was anticipated by Alvin Toffler in 1970.[49] But the post-industrial era spurned it in practice. So while print manufacturing technology has existed since the 1970s, post-industrialism focused on public sector jobs rather than the quaternary economy. The hobbyist embrace of print technology in the last decade though has opened up many ingenious applications of the technology. Consumer, retail and small business 'protoduction' markets seem plausible in a way that they were not 40 years ago. The development of short-run tailored production on a large scale appears more likely in the medium-term future than in the post-industrial past.

Anderson talks about a new industrial epoch.[50] This era is defined not by what you can buy in the conventional mass market but rather in a cross-over mass-specialist 'protoduction' market. This kind of quaternary market is based not on production runs of millions but rather on millions of small production runs. The economic value of such runs lies not in the relative cheapness of the product but rather in the rarity of the design of the product. Such design caters to a specific purpose or taste. Design-intensive manufacturers produce one or a handful or hundreds or even thousands of units of an item. But they do not produce millions. The smaller of these businesses do not even have to set up a factory to manufacture their products; they can create design files that a generic factory then prints out or cuts out. Entry costs to manufacturing thereby are significantly lowered. Barriers to production are reduced. The culture of making has a chance once more to expand, though this time not as a secondary industry but rather as a quaternary industry. Quaternary industries bring the consumer and the producer into a closer relationship. Prosumer behaviours are the commercial equivalent of the quantum qubit.

Human beings are innate makers. They are objectivating creatures. They have an impulsion to create things. Their myths and religions are about creation. They fill their world with the objects and artifices that they make: clothing, jewellery, furniture, machines and art objects. There are two kinds of quaternary maker businesses: replicant businesses and design-focused businesses. The first recreate old objects; the second create original, distinctive, rare or personalized objects. Having a problem finding a replacement for a screw whose head has been severed? Your hardware store does not stock it? So scan its twin and print it out. One day soon consumers will do this with their own desktop printers or else they will go down to a local print manufacturing shop with a USB stick to do it. Armies will print out broken parts on the battlefield. Need to fix a plane to get it back in the air? Replicant technology will manufacture the needed components on the spot.

All sorts of businesses will develop around this technology. The spare parts business in the auto industry is huge. It is almost as big as the source industry itself. Why order and ship a spare part when its file can be downloaded and printed or the object can be scanned and reverse engineered? Anderson cites the case of Nathan Seidle's Colorado firm SparkFun that manufactures small batches of hard-to-find electronic parts.[51] This kind of low-volume, high-margin business represents the heart of replicant capitalism. Its consumers are not in the market for a cheap part but rather for a scarce high-margin part. Sometimes they will pay almost anything for it. In the replica-part business, an old phased-out component can be expertly scanned to a design file and the file emailed to the consumer. Alternatively, the replicant part can be printed out and posted to the customer.

Design capitalism is a step beyond replicant capitalism. It focuses on original or personal creations. Want a stylish, distinctively designed, knife-and-fork set? Interested consumers will be able to licence an appealing design for a small fee and then print out the artefact. The design firm *i.materialize* calls this 'the power of the unique'.[52] Of course, the greater the number of fee-paying downloads, the less unique to the consumer the object will be. So then a market for limited edition designs will grow. Do you have a desire for a boutique car that incorporates your own design input? No problem: in the United States, you can already go to the Local Motors 3D printed cars site. The manufacturer in 2014 could print a car in 40 hours composed of 40 components using two technicians. The car designs are the co-creations of the producer, the consumer and the firm's 150,000-strong online community. This does not mean that the traditional mass manufacture of cars will disappear. Rather what the 3D car points to is the incremental growth of quaternary industries that embody a DIY component.

Anderson stresses the role of web-based online open source design communities in product development. He is sceptical about relying on closed source intellectual property. His vision is closer to the classic pre-1970 science university model of research or even the early days of Henry Ford's enterprise than it is to the post-industrial model preoccupied with intellectual capital. Anderson emphasises the value created by shared 'design' rather than by patented 'knowledge'. This model of design capitalism is different from a knowledge economy. It is not reliant on the licencing of patents. It is notable that, as the big bureaucratized legal-rational post-industrial organizations, from pharmaceutical corporations to universities, went down the intellectual property path, their real research and development output declined.[53]

Anderson's model makes sense for businesses focused on unique or personalized designs or on the intellectual gift economy of maker communities. That though has a limited application in the general economy where uniqueness or altruism is a less common motive. Some businesses can run successfully on romantic or altruistic premises. Most cannot. So maker platforms like Thingiverse will eventually look less like hobbyist sites and more like the commercial image broker Shutterstock, where consumers download stock images on demand for a fee. Maker files will be downloaded in the same way. We are not at that point yet. The maker movement is in its hobbyist phase right now. It is like the Homebrew-style personal computer movement in the 1980s. None the less as consumer and retail 3D printing grows, IP-driven small and medium businesses will develop around the technology along with stores for consumers to print out food designs, clothing designs, instrument designs, indeed almost any conceivable object they desire.

NOTES

1. Conversely today in the quaternary economy, home gardening is a major growth segment.
2. Haksever and Render (2013: 7).
3. BLS, all employees, thousands, manufacturing, seasonally adjusted time series CES3000000001.
4. CEDA (2015: 99).

5. Kenny (2014).
6. Baily and Bosworth (2014, figure 1). See also Perry (2012).
7. Haksever and Render (2013: 7).
8. Kenny (2014).
9. World Bank data, services, etc., value added (percentage of GDP).
10. Summers (2010).
11. World Bank data, services, etc., value added (percentage of GDP).
12. 'Quaternary' is sometimes used as a term for the information industries. The word is used differently in the current study, for those layers of the economy where the key driver is not information but rather autonomy.
13. Employment Projections program, US BLS, employment projections tables.
14. This figure is sharply down from the 10.5 percent projection of the 2012–22 BLS Employment Projections program, Table 1 Employment by major occupational group, 2012 and projected 2022.
15. US Census Bureau 2012, National Population Projections.
16. John Dragovits, the chief financial officer of Dallas-based Parkland Health and Hospital System, noted in 2012: 'If you look at an average hospital's financial statement, 50%–60% of their expenses are salaries and benefits. By definition healthcare is an inflationary model, but it's exacerbated by the fact that everyone wants to hire more people rather than think about how they can live with fewer people … The challenge in this industry has always been getting people excited and intrigued and rewarded for looking at things innovatively and using technology to do things quicker and cheaper.' Betbeze (2012).
17. Murphy (2015a: 16–18).
18. Fast-growing here is defined as businesses whose revenue growth was 3 percent per annum or higher compared with the average US GDP growth during these years of 2.5 percent. Ibis Industry Market Research Reports. Figures used are for 2010–15 unless otherwise noted.
19. BLS Employment Projections.
20. Friedman and Mandelbaum (2011); Brynjolfsson and McAfee (2014); Cowen (2013).
21. BLS, all employees, thousands, motor vehicles and parts, seasonally adjusted 1990–2016.
22. Moura, Smith and Belzer (2015). For purposes of comparison, internationally the average residential floor space per capita in square metres is: Hong Kong 15, France 43, Canada 72, Japan 35, United Kingdom 33, China 20, Denmark 65, Australia 89, Germany 55, Sweden 40, Italy 33, Greece 45, Spain 35 and Russia 22. Shrinkthatfootprint.com, 'How big is a house'.
23. BLS Employment Projections program, Table 1.7 Occupational employment and job openings data, projected 2012–22 and worker characteristics, 2012.
24. Deloitte (2014: 15). The report draws extensively on the research of Carl Benedikt Frey and Michael Osborne.
25. Deloitte (2015a, 2015b).

26. Deloitte (2015b, table 1).
27. In the noughties, the iphone and pro-am video camera killed off much of the traditional business for professional photographers, but new DIY markets have arisen in the aftermath of this with professional photographers offering short courses for serious amateurs, leading photography travel groups, and creating customized print-on-demand photographic books to showcase photos taken by amateur photographers. In each of these cases the product or service is co-created by the consumer. Consumer participation in the creation of the product is central to the economic value of the product.
28. The term prosumer was coined by Alvin Toffler (1980). It is someone who has the dual character of consumer and producer and who contributes to shaping the product that is consumed.
29. Gerhardt (2008).
30. Gerhardt (2008: 3).
31. Toffler (1980).
32. The many examples of highly accomplished college dropouts include Paul Allen, John Cage, Michael Dell, Bob Dylan, Larry Ellison, William Faulkner, Robert Frost, Bill Gates, Robert Hughes, Wayne Huizenga, Steve Jobs, Dean Kamen, Ralph Lauren, William McKinley, Tom Monaghan, James Monroe, Edgar Allen Poe, John D. Rockefeller, Karl Rove, Muriel Siebert, Steven Spielberg, Nikola Tesla, Ted Turner and George Westinghouse. Autodidactic.com, Profiles.
33. Nelson (2013).
34. Yoon (2013).
35. McCarthy (2015); ShareSoc (2016).
36. Statista, Value of the home improvement products market in the United States from 2011 to 2016.
37. Ibis (December 2015).
38. In February 2016, Facebook, Twitter and LinkedIn had between them a total share market capitalization of $320 billion. (AppraisalEconomics 2015 reviewed the market capitalization of such companies based on their 2014 share market valuations.) The Uber and AirBnB platforms, supporting self-employed owner-drivers and the peer-to-peer accommodation industry, in 2015 were estimated to be worth $62 billion and $20 billion, respectively; Newcomer (2015); Saitto (2015).
39. NoAgenda Homeschool (2012).
40. Ibis (August 2015).
41. Bowker (2014); Jones (2015). This is a platform-driven business. Major players include the Pearson-owned Author Solutions and Amazon-owned CreateSpace.
42. Leonard (2012). 'Interest in quilting, other forms of sewing and many crafts in general is increasing. At least one project a year is crafted in about 56 percent of American households, according to the Craft & Hobby Association, and the industry held steady at nearly $30 billion in annual revenue through the recession, when many other retail sectors declined.'

43. Ibis Industry Market Research.
44. Davidson (2015); Fromm (2013); Grose (2013). Millennials (Generation Y) are those born between 1980 and 2000.
45. Ibis (January 2016). The US electronics chain, Radio Shack, filed for Chapter 11 bankruptcy protection in 2015. In 2016, Australia's Dick Smith consumer electronics retailer chain was put into administration by its creditors.
46. Object-making has a conservative bias. This is apparent from political patterns in the online world. Conservatives, notably women, gravitate to Pinterest, the image upload site that catalogues 'things to do'. The site contains a lot of images of DIY and women's maker objects. Instagram, Google, Twitter and Reddit users lean politically to the left. Disqus, Bing, Yahoo and Pinterest users lean to the centre-right. Quantcast (2014).
47. Anderson (2012).
48. Anderson (2012: 8–9, 14, 24, 97).
49. Toffler (1970).
50. Anderson (2012: 17–31).
51. Anderson (2012: 160–2).
52. Anderson (2012: 67).
53. Murphy (2015a, 2015c).

3

PUBLIC GOODS

POST-INDUSTRIAL TO AUTO-INDUSTRIAL

It is hard to say exactly what occupations a future auto-industrial society will generate. Governments doubtless will be tempted to try and create ever more post-industrial jobs in an era when the need and demand for such jobs is declining. The limit of this is clear. Governments rely on budgets that depend on the underlying real economy. The wider economy produces the tax revenues that are the financial lifeblood of government. If the real economy shrinks so does the government's tax base. Public finances ultimately depend on private finances. The success of the future real economy depends on it making an effective transition from post-industrialism to auto-industrialism. The best contribution that governments can make to this transition is fiscal restraint. Funding declining post-industrial jobs by means of debt, deficits or higher taxes is necessarily counterproductive. The condition of an expanding quaternary economy will be a leaner post-industrial sector. In a productivity-driven economy there is no growth without accompanying trimming.

This applies as much to the core activities of government as anything. Quaternary growth will require governments to employ auto-industrial techniques to reduce the size of government. This is the polar opposite of the post-industrial approach. Many of the highest growth occupations in the post-industrial era were public sector jobs. Accordingly, in most advanced economies public finance as a share of real GDP grew significantly. It is unexceptional today in major economies for 40 percent of GDP to be expended by government (at all levels). Estimates of the optimal level of government spending range from 17 percent to 30 percent of GDP.[1] The optimal level is that which is conducive to a high rate of economic growth.[2] The post-industrial era saw government spending typically rise in the major economies.

Governments taxed and borrowed in order to expand their bureaucracies, services and transfer payments.

A classic example of this was higher education. The single most costly public good today is a university education. In the post-industrial era the real cost of higher education grew four-fold.[3] Powerful post-industrial lobbies emerged that even today continue to agitate for ever-larger public subsidies for higher education. The main effect of public subsidies is to drive up the price of public goods. The logic of auto-industrialism points in the opposite direction.[4] This is in part because of the changing nature of work. Today there is declining need for graduates from the mass university system. This system was geared to 'knowledge work'. This kind of work is gradually being replaced by machines. Many of the sales-and-office occupations that characterized the post-industrial economies are beginning to disappear. Beneath the surface of this development lie some potent historical ironies.

Technology shapes employment. That is the norm of industrial societies. Post-industrial society shed a lot of occupations. It exported manufacturing work abroad or else automated it. When manufacturing's share of employment declined in the United States, many of its employees experienced cuts in real income or fell into unemployment ending up on disability pensions or in lower-level service jobs. Post-industrialism created a social structure composed of a postgraduate elite notable for its superciliousness and moralizing; a white-collar graduate middle class that performed routine officework; a declining blue-collar industrial class; and a low-income class doing service and manual work. The white-collar and blue-collar middle class experienced stagnant real incomes together with the spiralling costs of public goods managed by the postgraduate class. Notable was the soaring real cost of health and education. In the United States, education tuition costs rose 300 percent between 1990 and 2011; health costs rose 150 percent; inflation rose 75 percent.

These financial pressures were compounded by the rise in housing costs in the post-industrial era. The median inflation-adjusted price of US dwellings increased four-fold between 1940 and 2000. The price in real terms of new dwellings doubled between 1995 and 2007.[5] In Australia nominal average wages rose 13-fold between 1973 and 2014 while the nominal cost of housing rose 30-fold.[6] In real terms, that represents a 1.4-fold increase in real incomes and a three-fold increase in real housing costs. In Australia's case, at least in the 1980s, house prices mirrored general price inflation. However, from 1990 onwards house prices exceeded general inflation. House prices increased 7 percent p.a. between 1990 and 2005; and 5 percent p.a. between 2006 and 2015. General price inflation was in the 2 to 3 percent p.a. range. The Reserve Bank of

Australia (RBA) discounts the notion that inflated house prices can be explained by increased house building quality and size.[7] The RBA argues rather that high house price inflation was caused by a combination of low interest rate-fuelled overdemand and the undersupply of buildings. After 1990, Australia's dwelling price-to-income ratio rose as household debt-to-income rose. In other words cheaper credit made houses more expensive. Too much money chased too few houses. A crucial factor in this was the undersupply of housing. As demand increased the production of new housing remained constant. The reason for this (arguably) was regulation. Supply side rigidities, the RBA observes, were caused by government planning and zoning policies. Regulation created an artificial housing scarcity.

The post-industrial era saw the prices of housing, health and education rise in the major economies. This was offset if only to a degree by the steadily declining prices of globalized manufactured goods and the ever-decreasing prices of IT. A washing machine that cost a median American employee 48.5 hours of working time in 1981 cost 26.7 hours of working time in 2013.[8] The future requires the kind of automation that can reduce public good costs in the same way that white goods costs have been reduced across the past half century.[9]

This implies a sustained reduction in the high cost of big government-style regulatory-health-and-education goods. The technologies of the post-industrial era, much praised by the postgraduate class, are beginning now to slowly devour the office empires of that same class. Mid-tier, post-industrial, white-collar and pink-collar work is starting to go the way of the old industrial blue-collar jobs. Such work is being mechanized, robotized, subject to algorithms, automated, computerized, programmed and increasingly eliminated. The jobs that are likely to dominate in the auto-industrial age will have unprogrammable 'character'. Many and probably most of these character jobs will still be com-puter-mediated. The human–machine interface, already commonplace, will continue to grow in importance. Machines are inescapable. If you do not like machines or do not like interacting with them then finding a comfortable place in an industrial society is difficult.

What is clear is that the number of 'if-then' jobs is in decline and has been for some time. The employment structure of advanced economies is polariz-ing.[10] Employment is gravitating to the high-skill and low-skill ends of the job spectrum.[11] Mid-skill and middle-income jobs are shrinking. This shrinkage will continue in the foreseeable near term. In the longer term, whether advanced economies can grow mid-skill jobs again depends on whether or not the mid-level 'if-then' jobs can be replaced by mid-range kinds of capital work along with 'as if' occupations and problem-solving roles.

The latter assumes a major spontaneous social adaptation. It cannot be engineered by government policy, training schemes, skills development and education — or any of the conventional government-funded human capital strategies of the post-industrial era.[12] This is because the very nature of work is up for grabs. Human capital strategies assume that education produces jobs and that the role of education (including that of higher education) is to produce a mass administrative workforce capable of the kind of symbol manipulation that is used in document-based process work (financial, legal, technical, HR, management, marketing and so on). This is what is called 'knowledge work'. Such work is being automated. Such automation has been happening incrementally at least since 1990.

Consequently the need for mid-skill white-collar office work, much of it located in the public sector, is declining. Only if there is a demand for alternate kinds of mid-tier jobs can the effects of this be reversed. The problem is that this also requires a cultural shift. It means undoing all kinds of widespread post-industrial and human capital assumptions. It means rethinking mid-tier work in terms of capital work, pattern work, character work and occupations in the quaternary sector of the economy. It also means rethinking education in its entirety, as it has been fixated for the past four decades on the idea of a 'knowledge economy'. Auto-industrial era education (education for autonomy) is necessarily different in nature from the kind of mass higher education and bureaucratically organized primary and secondary education that ballooned after 1970. The future is not a *fait accompli*. The number of analogizing 'as if' occupations might or might not grow depending on whether advanced societies adapt themselves to new realities or not.

What is clear from the experience of the past decades is that post-industrial societies paid a heavy price for the number of 'if-then' jobs that those societies created. The formula of 'a university degree = a white-collar job' was costly and the social dividend that it paid declined over time. Post-industrialism initially was a response to the export of manufacturing jobs overseas. With those jobs went middle-income work. Median wage incomes tended to flatten during the post-industrial era as persons transitioned from manufacturing to office, sales and service jobs. Since 1990, office-and-sales jobs have started to decline. Jobs have gradually polarized between low-income service work and high-income postgraduate work.

The effect of this on the standard of living in advanced economies has been cushioned by the growing cheapness of consumer goods (cars, clothes, cell phones, TVs) imported from newly industrialized countries. The resulting fall in the prices of white goods in part compensated for stagnant or declining incomes.

What this could not offset though was the spiralling cost of post-industrial regulatory, health and education goods. In real terms the cost of these ballooned. This cost spiral was caused by the compulsive bureaucratization of post-industrial societies.

In the 1970s and 1980s, to compensate for the declining industrial, blue-collar, mid-tier jobs, governments willed into existence phalanxes of white-collar and pink-collar 'if-then' workers. Document-and-rule production grew. Through the 1990s and the noughties, effective demand for mid-tier corporate white-collar employment fell along with employment in the classic nightwatchman components of the state. In 1970, the United Kingdom spent 5.42 percent of its GDP on defence; by 2015, the figure had fallen to 2.47 percent. At the same time government debt and deficits financed a large growth in health and education employment. Between 1970 and 2015, health and education spending in the United Kingdom rose from 9.41 percent of GDP to 11.38 percent. In 1961 in the United Kingdom, public sector employees in the National Health Service and education totalled 2.4 percent of the population. By 2013 the figure had grown to 5 percent.[13] In the United States, public health expenditure (measured in constant 2014 dollars terms) swelled more than three-fold from $1,700 per capita in 1995 to $4,512 in 2014.[14]

Bureaucracy was a key driver of post-industrial public expenditure. A typical example is the case of public health spending in Australia. In Queensland in 1995–96 there were 0.21 managers and administrators for every health practitioner (doctor, nurse, or technician) in the Queensland state health system; in 2011–12, the figure was 0.31. Nationwide in 2015 there was one administrator for every 3.4 hospital beds.[15] Foreseeably in the auto-industrial era, a new equilibrium of factors will dominate. This will entail fewer 'if-then' jobs and a gradual increase in the number of jobs in the quaternary sector of the economy combined with still cheaper consumer goods and (crucially) lower-priced housing and public goods.

In this social environment, 'cost of living' and 'cost of government' are likely to be key political economy factors. Auto-industrialism implies that government, health and education services are a lot less costly to deliver. This requires a revolution in the conception of public goods and the regulation of social goods. Essentially, it means removing the large administrative and regulatory overheads that drive up the price of housing, health and education in advanced economies. This will be contested. Post-industrial ideologies have been a prime justification for the bureaucratization of society. The mass university provided the resulting bureaucratic society with certified labour. The universities, in their turn, became massively bureaucratized. Any effective political economy in the future, of necessity, will have to correct this. Any correction will be strongly resisted. With the demise of mass industrialism the only effective sector of the modern union movement that is left are the public sector unions.

The auto-industrial era will not provide large numbers of mid-tier, mid-income 'if-then' jobs. The demand for routine manual and service work is reducing. Foreseeably capital work, analogical work and character work will expand. New industries based on new technologies are likely to emerge as they have done in the past. But since the end of the classic manufacturing era in which big factories employed large skilled and semi-skilled workforces, new industries (excluding the public sector) have produced fewer mid-tier 'if-then' jobs than did their predecessors (the nineteenth-century railways and the twentieth-century automobile industry). In the post-industrial era, as has been noted, median incomes flatlined. High-level professional incomes increased as did the return from capital (income in the form of profits, rents, interest, royalties, dividends and the like).

As post-industrial sales-and-office work declines, household-based ('electronic cottage'-style) work will grow. Electronic platforms allow increased use of household capital for productive income-generating purposes. As the office-based, white-collar and pink-collar workforce declines, this decline will be offset by the continuing growth in the quaternary autonomous economy. As both a cause and effect of this, we can expect to see the hyper-regulation of the post-industrial state reduce. A logical condition of the autonomous economy is the rolling back of an oversized state that cannot but interfere with autonomous behaviour simply because many jobs in the state only exist in order to produce administrative rules that limit human autonomy. Less administration implies greater autonomy. The growth of the quaternary economy thus assumes the existence of a smaller state and limited government.

Post-industrial societies expanded the size of the state. The enlarged state did two things. First, it redistributed income. That is, it transferred income from middle and upper income strata to persons who were not employed or else were only marginally employed. Transfer payments now typically exceed spending on the core traditional nightwatchman functions of the state (that is, on law and defence). In 1960 the UK government spent 8 percent of public money on pensions and 19 percent on defence. In 2016 it allocated 6 percent for defence and 20 percent for pensions, an effective reversal of spending priorities.[16] Second, the post-industrial state grew health-and-education jobs but reduced police-defence-and-public-administration jobs relative to population. Auto-industrialism, it is expected, will continue the latter trend. Models for the automation of warfare and security have been developing rapidly as have schemes for the automation of government administration.[17] Over the long term these should have a real effect. In addition the expansive post-industrial health-and-education empires are not immune from auto-industrialization. One UK example will suffice to illustrate. From 1994 to 2010, primary and secondary teaching jobs in the United Kingdom grew by 30 percent. The number of teaching assistants grew by 400 percent.[18] Any job labelled 'assistant' is highly likely to be automated in the future.

CUTTING THE COST OF GOVERNMENT

The history of industrial capitalism is a history of cycles.[19] Capitalism does not function in a linear manner. Industries rise and fall — and they do so simultaneously, rising as they fall.[20] Established industries decline as new industries materialize. We saw this in the 1970s and 1980s. Manufacturing industries in advanced economies contracted sharply as the information industries began to appear. Growth accompanied shrinkage — and shrinkage accompanied growth. The story of the post-industrial era though was less than salutary. For the IT industries did not produce the same numbers of jobs that were lost as manufacturing declined. None of the successive generations of information industries (from mainframe to personal computing to social media) compare with the employment capacity of the early- and mid-twentieth-century car industry for example. The principal employment growth in the post-industrial era was in services. Office-and-service jobs scaled to 70–80 percent of employment in the advanced economies. The most striking thing about these jobs, as they expanded, was how resistant they were to productivity improvements.

While work in the tertiary industries escalated, these jobs saw little improvement in productivity over time. Contrast this with primary and secondary industries. As technology was added to the latter sectors, output per capita rose significantly. Fewer hands were needed to produce more goods. Consequently, the price of foodstuffs fell sharply across the course of the twentieth century; manufactured goods even more sharply. The price of services did not.[21] In the case of public goods they rose. Education and health services were much more costly at the end of the twentieth century than they were in the middle of the twentieth century. And as their prices rose, their quality declined. Lower prices in real terms for primary and secondary goods meant increased consumer purchasing power — making nominal income go further. Provision of tertiary services had the converse effect. The increasing numbers of jobs in the tertiary sector was accompanied by low productivity gains in that sector. From 1990 onwards, the sector was computerized. Yet productivity improvement was generally minimal and limited mostly to the 1995–2000 period.

In fact in many areas computers drove the expansion of paperwork. They made bureaucratic routine more pervasive and communicable. The term 'service' was a misnomer. In many instances it was a euphemism for administration. For every frontline tertiary sector employee, a back office administrator of some kind was employed. Frontline work itself was consumed by paperwork demands.[22] This was the antithesis of the productivity revolution that occurred in the manufacturing industry.

As jobs declined in manufacturing they expanded in tertiary sector bureaucracies. Pink-collar and white-collar work surged as did various kinds of para-professions. Assistants, support personnel, aides, deputies, secretaries, advisors, administrators, clerical workers, officials, managers, auditors, executives, directors and officeholders of a seemingly infinite variety proliferated. They legitimated themselves and their occupations by claiming that they delivered valuable things called 'education' or 'health' venerated by society. What they actually delivered was process: most of this was a creature of internal organizational policy and external administrative regulation — and most of it was an encumbrance on the 'service' it purported to enhance.[23]

The spiralling price of public goods since 1970 has meant that these goods increasingly have been funded by government deficits and debts. In major economies, this has been in spite of a shrinking number of persons who actually pay tax and in spite of the aging profile of national workforces. In 1970 in the United States, seven employees supported every retiree; today it is four. In 2050, it will be two employees. This is not sustainable. Among the most expensive consumer items today are health and education. Both attract direct and indirect government subsidization. The more that governments subsidize these goods, the greater the real cost of these goods becomes. This then fuels demands for increased subsidization that then drives ever higher prices for these goods. The spiral is vicious. In the mid-1960s, US governments spent 1 percent of GDP on healthcare; in 2012 it was 7.9 percent. Total healthcare spending as a share of GDP grew from 9 percent of GDP in 1980 to 16 percent in 2012.

The proximate causes of this were various: overuse of diagnostic technology, excessive pricing by suppliers, overservicing of patients, overgenerous hospital union contracts and pensions, a maze of compliance demands, and physicians and patients who have little or no responsibility for costs incurred. But the root cause of the spiralling costs was government itself. The more governments spend on public goods, the more that costs and prices go up. The intent of government is to reduce costs to consumers by sharing costs; the effect of subsidies however is to drive costs up, leaving consumers worse off. A higher education today costs in real terms four times what it cost in the 1950s.[24] Even with government subsidies deducted from the price, it costs 2.5 times what it cost in the 1950s.

Is it any wonder that national healthcare costs are what they are?[25] In Australia between 1990 and 2014 the total real costs per person of healthcare rose 2.3-fold. Individual non-government health costs rose 4.1-fold.[26] What explains this? There was a technology and aging population component in this. Even so, in principle technology should be cost-reducing as much as cost-increasing and older populations while sicker should be reaping the advantages of the billions that have been spent on preventive healthcare over their lifetime. What the large cost increase points to is the systemic resistance of the post-industrial public goods sector to productivity gains. The obverse of this is that the health industry is beset by over pricing, over servicing, inefficiency, time wasting, bureaucracy, committees and a general lack of delivery competition and innovation.

The post-industrial health sector suffers from over-regulation, pointless auditing, escalating paperwork for practitioners, the replacement of vocational ethics by procedural rules, the lack of effective cost reduction incentives, the insuring of non-insurable events (like routine doctors' visits), the public funding of excessive medical consultations, the political equation of more spending with better services, overcharging, overtesting, overstaffing, medico-legal over-investigation, the proliferation of administrative staff relative to practitioners, the use of labour-intensive procedures instead of automation, poor scheduling resulting in time wasting, the underutilization of resources, bureaucratic rationalizations aimed at notional efficiencies that actually increase costs, delivery time consumed by meetings, unionized staff working to rule, opaque funding rules and costly organizational rebadging.

The ultimate underlying driver of all of this is the government subsidization of healthcare. Subsidization is designed to make things cheaper for the consumer. Yet intentions are not the same as consequences. Whenever governments subsidize goods or services their real cost increases rather than reduces. This is because subsidization guarantees a flow of revenue to providers without those providers having to do anything except put up their prices.

In the nineteenth century, the era of the nightwatchman state, 10 percent of national income in major economies went to taxation. Principally this paid for the state to provide the system of laws, courts, police and defence. Today in leading states 30–50 percent of national income is absorbed in taxation.

Commonly today, states spend 10 percent of national income on health and education; 10–20 percent on pensions, unemployment benefits and other transfer payments; and 10 percent on law and defence.[27] Alongside governments, private organizations and foundations are also deeply involved in the provision of public goods. Nowadays little distinguishes between the culture of the public hospital and the private hospital; or the state university and the private university. All have the same bureaucratic 'service' culture. All are deeply mired in a post-industrial ethos that is obsessed with internal and external regulation and compliance.[28] All focus on document production and rule compliance.[29]

The preoccupation with process in one sense is understandable. This is 'where the jobs are' — or at least have been. Unions were once dominated by the private manufacturing sector; today they are dominated by the public sector. This has meant that post-industrial service and office work is mythologized as 'vital'. For when such work evaporates, there is not an obvious replacement for it. Consequently the rhetoric that surrounds it presents it as indispensable. The thing, though: it is not. The bureaucratic functions that have attached themselves to 'health and education' are not essential. Their necessity arises only from the imperatives of an organizational culture that defines bureaucratic processes as cardinal. The mentality of this procedural culture supposes that life, limb, sanity and all things fundamental hinge on employees who follow 'procedure and policy'. Each procedural step adds labour.

Auto-industrialization promises productivity increases in traditionally low productivity sectors. Most compliance functions are in principle computable. They can be automated. In practice though public sector IT systems tend to be systemically dysfunctional. The failure of the Australian Bureau of Statistics computers on census night 2016, with millions of users denied access, illustrates the point. The debacle of the Obamacare Healthcare.gov IT roll-out in 2013 in the United States is typical of a sector that resists automation.[30] Likewise the massive theft of personal data from the Obama administration's Office of Personnel Management in 2015. Data on an estimated 18 million personnel was stolen in a cyber breach. President Obama excelled at using data mining techniques in campaigning for political office. Yet as an advocate of big government, his administration was visibly disinterested in effective IT automation. This kind of disinterest is a recurring feature of contemporary big government. In 2014, American corporations reported 26 major data breaches.[31] There are one million large corporations in the United States.[32] In the same year, the US federal government reported 23 major breaches.[33] There are 227 federal government agencies and departments.[34]

The difference between the private and public sector in the rate of breaches per organizational unit is breathtaking yet not surprising. For government to implement the type of effective IT that saves labour implies the shrinking of government as its routine processes and functions are automated. This defies the logic of big government to continuously expand. Ultimately this problem is not a matter of technology but of political will. Estonia's small-government-high-technology approach suggests that IT can be applied to government effectively.[35] However, to date, public sector IT in leading economies is typically hopeless.[36] Among the worst of its kind is university institutional IT.

Ian Duncan-Smith, at the time the United Kingdom's Work and Pensions Secretary, sought to introduce a Universal Credit system in 2013. The idea was a single tax credit to replace six existing state benefits and tax credits. Crucially the Universal Credit tapers. Accordingly, it encourages beneficiaries to pursue part-time work and so escape from the poverty trap of perpetual public benefits. The greatest problem faced in introducing this reform (still at the pilot stage in 2015) was the United Kingdom's public sector IT systems. These systems are marked by chaotic and inept operations — and attempts to improve them result in the chronic deferral of decisions.[37] Endless reviews and plans are sought in order to avoid action and implementation.[38]

Public sector IT aimed at efficiency and productivity today is mostly a contradiction in terms. This is because IT effectiveness brings sector shrinkage rather than expansion. Such shrinkage though cannot be resisted forever. Eventually limited public finances will force IT efficiencies on reluctant public sectors. Take the case of universities. These, today, have 70 percent overheads. They are cost-ineffective, price-gouging compliance leviathans. But in the foreseeable future some gifted individual will invent an effective digital platform for university administration.[39] At that point, the world will change. Academics, who today are in the main either state-funded or state-subsidized, will exit the prevailing bureaucratic form of university organization. Alternative lean organizations will emerge. These will assume, both technologically and culturally, a high level of self-organization, self-service and classic autonomy. The economics of this will be attractive to students, academics and taxpayers.

PUBLIC PRODUCTIVITY VERSUS TRANSFER PAYMENTS

If post-industrial computerization aided the rise of the bureaucratic service culture, auto-industrial technologies now promise to defenestrate that same culture. Office automation has the potential to generate major productivity gains in tertiary industries.[40] It has the capacity to reduce the high price of post-industrial education and health — making them affordable in a way that they are not today. The real prices and costs of health and education have escalated dramatically since 1970. One of the principal effects of the post-industrial era was to drive up the cost of education and health by loading up these public goods with elaborate bureaucracies and procedures. It is notable that studies single out 'administration and support services' as one of the principal areas being affected by contemporary automation. Accommodation and food services and transport services are in the first tier projected to be most heavily affected by automation. Administration and support services belong in the second tier along with real estate, retail, wholesale and manufacturing.[41]

Possibilities though are not realities. Post-modern bureaucracies will resist being replaced by intelligent machines. Every morsel of progressive rhetoric will be mobilized in this intransigent cause. Not only that, public sector administrations have a poor track record in implementing automated systems. The sector's IT historically in the main has worked to increase rather than decrease the bureaucratic burden on those involved in frontline delivery. In the United States, the Obama administration's mandated implementation of electronic health records increased rather than reduced paperwork. The underlying driver of this has little to do with technology. It is rather one of social class. Since 1970, a large bureaucratic class developed in both the public and private sectors. The function of this class is to deliver taxpayer-subsidized goods.[42] It does this in a manner that is almost inoculated against productivity increases.[43]

As an example, it utilizes IT not so as to reduce the labour-intensive handling of paperwork as might be expected but rather to increase it. It matters not that records are in an electronic form. That does not in itself make records-handling more efficient or less labour intensive. Rather the reverse applies. Whole new workforces arise as ever more detailed steps are added to new electronic procedures requiring additional sign-offs, audits, reviews and requests for further information. The post-modern bureaucratic class will not go away without a fight. It can bungle the introduction of automated systems. It can turn self-service into a nightmare of prolix, protracted and multiplying steps that extract mountains of needless details from users under the pretence of automation. Tardiness, deferral, postponement and lateness are the stock-in-trade of these bureaucracies. The spirit of this is the antithesis of economy. It requires not the least effort but the most effort.

That said, though, the spectre of automation continues to haunt governments. The Australian Government for example has been looking systematically at automated administrative decision-making support since 2004.[44] One of the original models for this was the Compensation Claims Processing System

(CCPS) introduced by Australia's Department of Veterans Affairs in 1994. This was a system for the investigation and determination of claims by veterans and their families. The decision support system was originally based on 2,000 pages of legislation and 9,700 rules. It covered all steps along the 'lodgement-of-claim to payment-of-support' path. It registered claims, recorded claimant details, checked claims against legal requirements for lodgement, checked that medical diagnoses met diagnostic criteria, investigated causes of conditions claimed, decided if conditions were linked to war service or defence service employment, assessed the rate of pension or amount of compensation, and notified the claimant of decisions and reasons for the decision. This did not replace the need for administrative judgement in complex cases but it assisted where the decision making involved had a clear algorithmic tree structure.[45]

The Australian Government claimed that after the CCPS was introduced, 30 percent fewer officers processed 30 percent more decisions annually. A web version of the CCPS, Military Compensation Expert, was introduced in 2004 based on 40 pages of legislation and 3,500 rules. Whether automated decision assistants can obviate the chronic post-modern multiplication of rules and pages of legislation is an open question. But it can reduce the human labour involved by reducing the need for human beings to endlessly repeat the same decision steps. Lobbies can still pressure lawmakers to add even more rules and legislative mandates, and ever more obscure rationales for making claims. White-collar robotics[46] cannot eliminate the work entailed by new entitlements or new procedures — but it can shrink the volume of human labour time involved in executing the seemingly ever-escalating ambitions of legislators and administrative regulators.

The bureaucratic class in advanced economies has grown to such a size that its scions constitute major lobbies inside and outside government. Government-subsidized actors place pressure on governments to expand the number of government-subsidized actors. Yet against these hot-house lobbies, governments also have to weigh growing fiscal problems. These manifest either as shrinking tax revenues or else the growth of taxation as a proportion of GDP. In the US government revenue as a share of GDP grew from 8 percent in 1900 to 13 percent in 1920, 18 percent in 1943, 25 percent in 1956, 30 percent in 1970 and 35 percent in 2014.[47] While the tax share of GDP has increased, GDP's rate of growth has decreased.

The days of mass industrialism are long past. Today the economic model of post-industrialism is exhausted. Economic growth in major economies is sluggish. The United States averaged an annual growth in real GDP of 3.6 percent between 1948 and 2000. That figure fell sharply to 1.7 percent between 2001 and 2014.[48]

As growth shrinks and spending increases, either tax revenues decline or the tax share of GDP grows.[49] To avoid this the temptation for governments is to substitute borrowings and debt for taxes. The US federal debt grew from $5.8 trillion in 2011 to $18.2 trillion in 2015. From 2001 to 2014, the US government borrowed $4 trillion more than the economy grew.[50]

This fiscal pattern is not sustainable. Yet old political habits die hard. Major states spend extensively on law-and-defence, transfer payments and education-and-health. In 2008, OECD countries spent 6 percent of their collective GDP on education. Chile, Denmark, Iceland, Israel, Korea, Norway and the United States spent more than 7 percent.[51] Health spending accounted for 16.9 percent of GDP in the United States in 2012. The rest of the OECD ranged between 11.8 percent (the Netherlands) and 5.4 percent (Turkey). Australia was 9.1 percent; the United Kingdom was 9.3 percent.[52] In many major economies, spending on health-and-education now exceeds 15 percent of national wealth.

It varies as to what share of that total is represented by government spending. In 1995, 45 percent of health spending in the United States was public expenditure. In 2014 that had grown to 48 percent. Over the same period the Australian government spending on health increased from 65 to 67 percent; the Netherlands 71 to 87 percent; Turkey 70 to 77 percent. The United Kingdom was constant at 83 percent. Across the world the figure rose from 56 to 59 percent.[53] The propensity of states to spend however is not matched by their capacity to pay for this spending. In the long term, the mismatch will either be the cause of sustained economic decline or else it will oblige states to rethink their approach to public goods. This in turn will require a hard look by governments at high-cost, high-priced public goods, particularly education and health.

If automation eliminates jobs, that is alright (so the argument runs): everyone can receive a guaranteed minimum income from the state. If persons do less work or no work or have no work for longer periods of time, they can be supported by transfer payments. But can they? Assuming that the amount of mid-tier 'if-then' work declines, how can such a redistributive transfer model be sustained? It is already under pressure. It relies heavily on taxing society's currently shrinking middle-income strata. Periodically the ideological chant of 'tax the wealthy' is heard. Not only is that affluent social tier already heavily taxed but a simple thought experiment demonstrates the limit of the taxation-and-redistribution paradigm.[54] Imagine if the entire wealth of the wealthiest 1 percent of society was redistributed equally to the rest of the society. If that happened, the real benefit to everyone else per head would be minuscule.[55]

The reality is that income tax redistribution only works if there is a substantial middle class reliably earning a good income. The number of persons securely in that category is declining and has been for some time. The only group in effect now positively contributing net tax (total tax paid less transfer payments received) to the US federal government is the top twenty percent of taxpayers.[56] This is a post-industrial phenomenon. It has affected most advanced economies, though not all.[57] Auto-industrialism to this point has also played a part in this decline. The consequence is that the salaried income tax base of states in major economies has contracted. To try and tax a declining tax base even more, only exacerbates the underlying problem. The core problem is the shrinkage of the middle-income, wage- and salary-earning social tier.

If that was the only factor in play then tomorrow will surely end up looking like Scotland does today. However, there are countervailing factors to be considered. Chief among these is that income is not only generated by wages and salaries. There is also the prospect of growing mid-tier income from capital — from rents, interest, profits, dividends and the like. People associate the term 'capital' with 'the wealthy'. But one of the likely scenarios of the auto-industrial age will be an increase in the relative weight of small and medium-sized businesses and an increase in the number of people who draw income not from wages or salaries but from capital. This is the model of popular capitalism or disintermediated capitalism. It is a social model that is latent in auto-industrial technologies.

It is impossible to predict with certainty that an increase in income from capital work will compensate for the decline in income accruing to mid-tier wages-and-salaries. In a future with fewer 'if-then' jobs, can the ownership of small-and-medium businesses counteract the slide in wage-and-salary remuneration? Can ownership and entrepreneurship offset the decline in the demand for qualified routine white-collar, blue-collar and pink-collar labour? This is possible though it is uncertain. The autonomous economy may re-energize the ranks of the middle strata. It may generate sufficient new sources of income to counteract the decline of traditional salaried jobs. In the auto-industrial age, occupation is likely to have more of the characteristics of capital than of labour.[58] Classic industrial society created many wage-employee occupations that produced physical artefacts. The logic of an auto-industrial society is to generate the kinds of occupations that require the ownership of machines and that involve the management and coordination of those machines and related human–machine interactions. Driverless trucks will eliminate the need for truck drivers but not for truck owners who will have to oversee autonomous machines driving thousands of miles robotically across continents. The source of income in this model is different from that of the transport driver on wages.

As the demand for routine labour of all kinds shrinks, there are still likely to be strata that lack occupation. This is the result not just of unemployment but also of underemployment including underemployment in low-paying jobs. So there will continue to be pressure on the state to compensate persons for systemic social underemployment and low incomes. The post-industrial sense of social entitlement shows no signs of declining even in generations today that, on current trends, are not going to be as well off as their parents' generation was. So how does the state cope? There is a limit to the amount of transfer payments. The limit is two-fold: first, the real size of the tax base; second, the countervailing demands on the state to pay for health-and-education and its traditional night-watchman functions of defence-and-law. States try and evade these limits by borrowing money, but that is an illusion. Borrowed money has to be repaid with interest. It only delays the inevitable reckoning. The point of reckoning is when spending exceeds revenue or when spending causes the state to choose between its pension-and-welfare, health-and-education and night-watchman functions.

An alternative is for the state to spend less and deliver more per dollar. This is the state equivalent of what happened to consumption in private life in the post-industrial age. Manufacturing work shrank and people turned to service work, which was less well paid. But 'less well paid' is a relative concept. For reduced nominal income under certain circumstances can still represent greater purchasing power. It depends on the real cost of goods. In the post-industrial era, it was possible to receive a lower nominal income but still enjoy a stable standard of living because the cost of many consumer items declined. The factories that produced these items were exported abroad to lower-wage countries that produced lower-cost goods that were exported to consumers in countries that formerly had large manufacturing industry workforces.

But this low-cost trend was then offset by a countervailing development in post-industrial societies. This was the bureaucratization of the delivery of public goods, notably health and education. These costs spiralled up dramatically. This was directly the consequence of increasing external compliance demands on these sectors and the internal drive of these sectors to bureaucratize themselves. They were subject to, and they subjected themselves to, a procedural fetish. The real costs per capita of public health-and-education goods escalated dramatically after 1970. One of the prime demands on the auto-industrial state will be to reduce the inflated cost of public goods. Lean public goods and shrunken regulation will be essential to ensuring that the algorithmic future does not mean a lower standard of living.

NOTES

1. Di Matteo (2013); Chobanov and Mladenova (2009); Tanzi (2005); Vedder and Gallaway (1998); Scully (1994); Peden (1991).
2. Economic performance is mirrored in government spending as a percentage of GDP. There is a strong correlation between lower spending as a percentage of GDP and long-run economic performance. The following list of government spending as a percentage of GDP doubles as a hierarchy of long-term economic dynamism: Hong Kong 17.6; Singapore 18.2; Taiwan 19.4; India 27; China 29.3; Switzerland 33.5; Australia 35.6; United States 38.9; Japan 42.3; Germany 44.3; United Kingdom 45.1; France 57. Heritage Foundation/*Wall Street Journal*, Index of Economic Freedom, 2016.
3. Murphy (2015a: 187–91).
4. Murphy (2016). No sector is immune from the wave of auto-production and auto-service. One day in the not-too-distant future, disintermediation will arrive at the door step of universities. The question will eventually arise as to why scholars need the agency of the bureaucratic university, a super-sized intermediary, to sell its wares, when a disintermediated process would allow students to directly purchase the services of a teacher or college of teachers without the current arrangement of the intermediary taking a 70 percent cut of the revenue to the teacher. The eighteenth-century university was disintermediated, and self-service software makes possible its return. This means that the 70 percent of income that currently goes to the agency of the university would shrink to a modest 20 percent as it was in the eighteenth century. The first beneficiary of this would be students who today pay tuition fees that are four times in real terms what they were in the 1950s. The second beneficiary would be the community of scholars. They would then deal directly with students sidestepping the current multitude of bureaucratic intermediaries and yet with the relative surety of algorithms. The disintermediated university, if it arrives, will be closer in nature to the *universitas magistrorum et scholarium*, the community of teachers and scholars, of the medieval era than to the mass bureaucratic university of the post-industrial age. This though is not medievalism warmed over. It is merely that change points as much to the past as it does to the future. But this is always a selective past. We are not about to see the revival of guilds, though doubtless some academics still hanker after them.
5. US Census Bureau, construction price indexes, historical data, price indexes for new single-family houses; historical census of housing tables, home values.
6. In 1973, median house prices across Australia's capital cities were: Sydney $27,400; Melbourne $19,800; Brisbane $17,500; Adelaide $16,250; Perth $18,850; Canberra $26,850; Hobart $15,200. The comparable September 2014 numbers from the Domain Group's House Price Report were: Sydney $843,994; Melbourne $615,068; Brisbane $473,924; Adelaide $459,258; Perth $604,822; Canberra $573,326; Hobart $322,274. Nominal prices increased around 30-fold. Wages increased 13-fold. In 1973, the average weekly wage was $111.80. In 2015, a full-time worker made on average $1,453 a week. See Domain.com blog, Australian-house-prices-then-and-now.

7. Kohler and van der Merwe (2015).
8. Perry (2013).
9. The following exemplifies health cost reduction via automation: Dallas-based Parkland Health and Hospital System reduced its headcount of financial counsellors from 200 to 130 by automating eligibility rechecks for patients who receive public assistance to pay for their medical care. Betbeze (2012).
10. The term 'polarization' was coined by Goos and Manning (2003).
11. Autor, Levy and Murnane (2003); Autor, Katz and Kearney (2006); Autor and Dorn (2013).
12. This is contrary to the view of the MIT economist David Autor, who has been a pioneer of the study of occupational polarization. Autor's human capital corrective (aka more education) to the phenomenon of occupational polarization is set out in Autor (2014) and Acemoglu and Autor (2012). Gordon (2016) makes roughly the same point proposing that 'we need to make a number of improvements in our educational system starting with much more widespread publically financed pre-school that goes down below ages four and three at least for the poverty population'. Sachs (2015) similarly advocates 'more government-supported education and training'. For those of left-liberal persuasion, all problems can be solved by education; all issues begin and end with an assertion of faith in knowledge. After a century of such assertions, it ought to be clear that such faith in knowledge is misplaced and education is not the universal solvent of all human problems, far from it.
13. Cribb, Disney and Sibieta (2014, figure 2a and 2b).
14. World Health Organization global health expenditure, health expenditure per capita (current US$) and health expenditure, public (percentage of total health expenditure). Total health expenditure per capita in the US in constant 2010 dollars rose from $3,788 (1995) to $9,403 (2014).
15. Creighton (2016).
16. ukpublicspending.co.uk
17. Auto-industrialism over the long term will reduce significantly the number of 'if-then' administrative jobs in the public and private sectors. That does not necessarily mean though in the first instance a reduction in the scale of state regulation but rather a change from the manual processing of compliance requirements to machines doing the work. As the size of the compliance workforce declines, the incessant lobbying for the expansion in the scale of regulation should begin to decline as well. A smaller compliance workforce will reduce the de facto lobby that constantly advocates for the expansion of regulation in order to expand the regulatory workforce.
18. Cribb, Disney and Sibieta (2014: 24).
19. Joseph Schumpeter thought this. When he published his two-volume work on *Business Cycles* in 1939, his former student and soon-to-be Keynesian superstar Paul Samuelson called it 'Pythagorean moonshine'. Keynesianism promised to counter cycles, subduing them with government intervention. That rarely happened. History proved Schumpeter right and Samuelson wrong. In the view of left-liberalism, nothing,

including the functioning of modern economies, was outside the power of human control. All that was required to control social outcomes were knowledge and policy expertise. That was an illusion of the age. A similar illusion of the age was minted when Samuelson predicted in the 1970 edition of his venerable textbook *Economics* that the GDP of the Soviet Union would exceed that of the United States in the 1990s. That prediction begged the question: who was drinking moonshine?

20. The view that modern societies are cyclical, not progressive, has deep intellectual roots. It goes back at least to the Roman thinker Polybius. Machiavelli revived the theme with his notion of 'circles of government'. James Burnham (1943) dubbed a group of early-twentieth-century thinkers (Michels, Pareto, Mosca) as 'the Machiavellian defenders of freedom' in part because they viewed history not as something progressive but rather cyclical. 'Political life, according to Machiavelli, is never static, but in continual change. There is no way of avoiding this change. Any idea of a perfect state, or even of a reasonably good state, much short of perfection, that could last indefinitely, is an illusion. The process of change is repetitive and roughly cyclical. That is to say, the pattern of change occurs again and again in history (so that, by studying the past, we learn also about the present and future); and this pattern comprises a more or less recognizable cycle. A good, flourishing, prosperous state becomes corrupt, evil, degenerate; from the corrupt, evil state again arises one that is strong and flourishing. The degeneration can, perhaps, be delayed; but Machiavelli has no confidence that it could be avoided. The very virtues of the good state contain the seeds of its own destruction.' Burnham (1943: 62). Something akin to this kind of circular motion also applies to modern industrial economies; they rise, fall, rise, fall.

21. Piketty (2014: 88–90).

22. The corollary (and often driver) of this was the managerial demand for compliance, short-term key performance indicators, bureaucratic empire-building within organizations and growing levels of micro-management.

23. As Hilton (2016) puts it: 'many of the services that centralised government provides — education, healthcare, social services, welfare — are well established and no longer require a centralised bureaucratic system to run them. Simply put, the raisons d'être of centralised government no longer justify it. But its costs remain.'

24. Murphy (2015a: 187–91).

25. Measured by 2008 OECD figures, Australia's healthcare costs were 8.5 percent of GDP; 17.7 percent of government revenue was spent on health; and government covered 67.5 percent of health costs. In the United States, the figures were 16.0 percent of GDP and 18.5 percent of government revenue for government coverage of 45.1 percent of health costs.

26. Per-person health expenditure in Australia rose in constant prices from $2,969 in 1989–90 to $6,637 in 2013–14; individual non-government spending per person rose from $515 to $2,137. Australian Institute of Health and Welfare (2016, tables A2 and A6). Individual spending represents a third of total health spending in Australia.

27. Piketty (2014: 475–9).
28. UK politician Nigel Farage's amusing observations on the changing work culture brought on by the cult of regulation: 'By the mid-1980s, I'd become a pretty good trader, broker and market-maker ... the Financial Services Act of 1986 ... introduced a regulatory culture of box-ticking, rather than leaving people with considerable financial expertise to police the City. It was the birth of a culture that would wreak financial devastation to our banking sector two decades later. The act brought in ghastly regulators who were supposed to police the City and make it safer for people to do business. But the vast majority of those regulators — God, I hate those people — had failed in the City. They just did not understand what bankers and brokers were up to. From 1986, I was asked to produce such things as risk assessments and would just refuse. It was like Health and Safety for derivatives. The whole point of the City is to take and manage risk and I had no intention of filling out a form to tell the compliance department — by then the fastest growing part of the business — how big the risk was. Compliance departments changed the whole culture of the City. Apart from monitoring everything, we had to start minding our Ps and Qs. They basically took the fun out of trading — and they also missed the point. While compliance departments were getting us all to tick boxes, they failed to register that a derivatives industry was growing exponentially under their noses, an industry dealing in products they did not understand and with a risk profile they were oblivious to.' Farage (2015).
29. Compliance is further incited by the insurance industry. It uses threats of higher premiums to force organizations to adopt stultifying risk-averse behaviours.
30. Two paradigmatic examples come from the Australian state of Victoria where the Bracks' State Labour government in the noughties oversaw two simultaneous IT disasters, the HealthSMART clinical ICT 'modernization' program and the MyKi smart card system. The resulting losses amounted to more than $1 billion in cost overruns. These matched in scale to California's ERP payroll software fiasco and the BBC's Digital Media Initiative debacle. Other notable examples of government IT failures include the FBI's 2001 Virtual Case File system, California's 1987–94 attempt to computerize its DMV, Canada's late 1990s national firearm registration computer system, and US Homeland Security's 2006 Secure Border Initiative Network.
31. Walters (2014).
32. US Census, number of tax returns and business receipts by size of receipts: 2000 to 2008, tables 744 and 745. In 2008 there were more than one million US corporations with receipts each of more than $1 million (and total receipts of over $26,000 billion).
33. Inserra and Rosenzweig (2014). Governments and businesses both underreport data breaches.
34. *United States Government Manual 2014*, Washington DC, US Government Printing Office, October 2014.
35. Cunliffe (2015) notes: 'Online voting isn't the only feature of the e-government that Estonians enjoy. Each citizen is assigned a unique ID number at birth, which they use for all official interactions, whether with government departments, or

with private companies which are integrated into the e-government system. They also have mandatory ID cards … which allows Estonian citizens to be recognised across government departments, without needing to sign up individually. Estonians each have a "digital signature", a unique cryptographic key which enables them to sign official contracts online … It is the integration between different systems that makes filling in tax returns so easy. Information concerning contracts, work permits, income, banking, pensions, charity donations, education and healthcare (to name but a few examples) is all linked to a citizen's ID number, meaning that, when they come to file their tax return, that information has already been included. All they need to do is check it is correct, and submit it — a process which takes 5 clicks … Advocates of small government should be paying close attention to Estonia. In an interview last month, the Prime Minister pointed out that "with the register of social securities, we are now building a new information system which allows us to do the same things with far fewer people, around 20 per cent less civil servants." According to Thomas Tamblyn … "The introduction of the digital identity alone saves the country two per cent of its annual GDP, and that's before you take into account the streamlining of each individual government service." And in terms of how much everything costs, Taavi Kotka, the undersecretary for information technology [at Estonia's Economy and Communications Ministry], has said that "All maintenance cost, salaries, investments together are around 50–60 million euros ($56–67 million), honestly." In comparison, the Obamacare website cost over $2 billion.' On Estonia's e-government, see also Dujmovic (2016); Sorrell (2015).

36. Inserra and Rosenzweig (2014) note some classic but hardly unusual examples of the chronic ineptness of US federal government IT: 'An April 2014 Government Accountability Office (GAO) report found that the IRS had "not always effectively implemented access and other controls to protect the confidentiality, integrity, and availability of its financial systems and information." The GAO concluded that financial and taxpayer information remained vulnerable to unauthorized access or threat. The IRS failed to install and update security patches, monitor database controls, and restrict mainframe access … The DOE [Department of Education] Inspector General's (IG) report for FY 2013 found the DOE was using unsecured networks. The IG reported that DOE was consistently not following IT security configuration procedures established by the National Institute of Standards and Technology, which meant that security patches often went without updates … Federal officials have known for over 6 years that Microsoft was going to end its support for Windows XP in April 2014. Despite that … about 10 percent of the 7 million computers used by the federal government still operated using Windows XP after public support ended.'

37. Johnston (2015).

38. Over 40 percent of IT failure is related to people issues; another 40 percent to process (scheduling, etc.) issues. One of the greatest people issues is problem employers. Government represents the problem employer par excellence for IT projects. Notably technology is rarely an issue in IT disasters. Nelson (2007).

39. Murphy (2016).
40. It costs a market survey firm one-tenth of the cost to do robotic opinion or market survey calls compared with employing survey personnel. Newell (2016).
41. Frey and Osborne (2015, figures 48, 60).
42. The new class of administrators was predicted by Burnham (1941).
43. In public and corporate bureaucracies, the size of the reporting team and the budget allocated to that team dictates the manager's place in the organizational status order.
44. Administrative Review Council (2004); Automated Assistance in Administrative Decision-Making Working Group (2007).
45. The Australian government (Automated Assistance in Administrative Decision-Making Working Group [2007, figure 1]) used the example of a customer who wants to hire a video from a video store. The automated system moves through a series of questions with yes/no answers and a decision tree that branches according to whether the answer is: yes or no. Along one branch, we begin with the question *is the customer a member of the video store*; if the answer is yes, then we move to the second question *does the customer have any unpaid late fees or overdue videos*; and if the answer is no, then the automatic decision of the system is that the customer can hire a video.
46. Ashton, Ashton and Davis (1994).
47. usgovernmentrevenue.com
48. US GDP growth percentages: 2015, 2.4; 2014, 2.4; 2013, 1.5; 2012, 2.2; 2011, 1.6; 2010, 2.5; 2009, –2.8; 2008, –0.3; 2007, 1.8; 2006, 2.7. Pethokoukis (2016).
49. In the period 1995 to 2014, government revenue as a share of GDP rose from 32.4 to 33.6 percent (Australia); 33.0 to 33.1 percent (United States); 31.1 to 35.8 percent (Japan); 36.1 to 38.2 percent (United Kingdom). In the same period, government debt as a percentage of GDP rose from 59.6 to 64.2 percent (Australia); 83.1 to 123.3 percent (United States); 93.8 to 239.8 percent (Japan); and 55.4 to 117.1 percent (United Kingdom). OECD, 'General government, 2015'.
50. Cost (2015).
51. OECD (2011).
52. OECD (2014).
53. World Health Organization global health expenditure, health expenditure, public (percentage of total health expenditure).
54. The top US marginal tax rate went from 70 percent under President Carter to 28 percent (Reagan), 40 percent (Clinton), 35 percent (G.W. Bush) and 39.6 percent (Obama). The US bottom 90 percent of income earners paid 50 percent of federal tax revenue in 1980 and 33 percent in 2011; the US top 1 percent of income recipients paid 19 percent of federal tax revenue in 1980 and 35 percent in 2011. The least that the bottom 90 percent ever contributed to federal government revenue (29 percent) was in 2007 (G.W. Bush). The contribution of the bottom 90 percent fell from 36 percent in 2001 (Clinton) to 29 percent in 2007 (G.W. Bush).

55. In 2013–14 tax year, the top 1 percent of US income earners earned $380,354 or above; the cohort paid $1,685,472 million in federal tax. Redistributed to every American that is $5,366 per head.

56. Congressional Budget Office, 2016. The second-highest quintile contributes only marginally more than it receives. The other three lower quintiles all receive more in transfers than they pay in tax.

57. 'A shift in the allocation of labor income towards the higher and lower ends of the distribution has resulted in a shrinkage of the income share accruing to the middle 20 percent in many advanced economies (Australia, Canada, and Sweden are important exceptions), and some large emerging market economies … Indeed, pre-tax incomes of middle-class households in the United States, the United Kingdom, and Japan have experienced declining or stagnant growth rates in recent years … In advanced economies, the largest driver has been the declining share of middle-skilled occupations relative to low- and high-skilled occupations.' Dabla-Norris, Kochhar, Suphaphiphat and Tsounta (2015).

58. Freeman (2015: 8) argues: 'Unless workers earn income from capital as well as from labor, the trend toward a more unequal income distribution is likely to continue, and the world will increasingly turn into a new form of economic feudalism. We have to widen the ownership of business capital if we hope to prevent such a polarization of our economies. There are diverse pathways to spread the ownership of capital. Ownership can take the form of worker assets in private pension funds or other collective savings vehicles that invest in shares on the stock market or that invest directly in equity in other firms. It can also take the form of workers buying shares or putting money in mutual funds themselves. But the form of ownership that potentially has the greatest economic benefit in dealing with robotization and the falling share of labor income is employee ownership. Employee ownership refers to the many mechanisms for workers to gain an ownership stake in their firm: through owning shares held by an employee ownership trust; through receiving stock options as part of their pay; through having part of their pay come in the form of profit sharing or other forms of group incentive pay; through being able to buy shares at low prices via employee stock purchase plans.'

CONCLUSION: THE AGE OF DIY CAPITALISM

DIY ECONOMIC GROWTH

There are signs that the organizational age, which began in the 1920s, is coming to an end. It was dominated by big companies, big government and big universities. Big companies are just as visible as ever. Yet measured against their capital size, they employ fewer people and they stay at the top of their league for shorter periods of time. Big government remains big but is beset by fiscal woes while big universities lack the gravitas and imagination of their smaller predecessors a hundred years ago. Smallness is on the agenda again.

Joel Kotkin observed that while unemployment in America surged after 2007, self-employment also grew.[1] A lot of people dropped out of the traditional labour market. Many exited into welfare but others stepped into work-at-home businesses. Sole trading plausibly is part of a future economic matrix that focuses on self-reliance, the converse of the post-industrial service model. This doubtlessly can be romanticized. Some yeoman enterprises succeed; others do not. From that hard-nosed point of view, the increase in the number of non-employer businesses in the post-2007 period was arguably just the flip side of the sharp decline of business start-ups in the United States. These were at their lowest number in 30 years. Yet such short-run pragmatics in fact appear to be overwritten by long-term structural developments that are causing a significant growth in micro and other small businesses in advanced economies. Factors facilitating this include the declining cost of capital and the capacity of the Internet to replace the coordination function of organizational hierarchies.

Analysing the rise of 'do-it-yourself economic growth', Heidi Pickman and Claudia Viek point out that the number of self-employed in the United States grew from 16 million in 2011 to 17.7 million in 2013 while the average size of new business start-ups fell from 7.6 employees in the 1990s to 4.7 employees in 2011.[2] As a share of US wage-and-salary employment, self-employment doubled between 1969 and 2009.[3] Even more tellingly, self-employment grew an average of 1.4 percent p.a. between 1969 and 2000. Then after 2000, as the post-industrial era began to power down, self-employment accelerated, growing at an average of 3.5 percent p.a. between 2000 and 2009. There is an element of back-to-the-future in all of this.[4] In 1880, 36.9 percent of Americans were self-employed. As the organizational era took off, that number shrank to 30.8 percent (1900), 23.5 percent (1920) and 18.8 percent (1939).[5] In 1948 the figure had declined to 18.5 percent of the work-force. A steep decline in self-employment occurred after the mid-1960s as the post-industrial era set in. By 2002, the self-employed workforce was down to 7.3 percent of the total. Then it rebounded. In 2013, it was 11 percent, back to the 1966 level.

A micro-business is a business with fewer than five employees or less than $50,000 start-up capital. Pickman and Viek note that in 2010 venture capital–backed companies accounted for 11.87 million jobs and over $3.1 trillion in revenue in the United States. In comparison micro-businesses were generating $2.4 trillion in receipts and employed more than 31 million people. One of the factors now contributing to the micro economy has been the rapid post-2008 expansion of platform capitalism. This is the phenomenon of Internet platforms that enable sole traders and home-based businesses to access large markets.[6] The online retailer Amazon was a pioneer of this. It provides an Internet plat-form for a large number of small businesses to sell goods and services through its site. Similar contemporary platforms include such as Uber (rides), Airbnb (home stays), Taskrabbit (chores), Instacart (grocery delivery), Homejoy (clean-ing services) and Postmate (deliveries). The freelance site Upwork enables clients to hire freelance business, engineering and design professionals. The site, started in 1999, reported $1 billion in billings in 2014.

Such platforms point to a distinct kind of capitalism. It can be described in many ways — popular capitalism, democratic capitalism, indie capitalism. It is a departure from the type of capitalism that prevailed during the age of organization that crystallized in the 1920s and 1930s. 1920–2010 was an era of institutional capitalism. It was dominated by large firms. These were bureau-cratically organized systems of offices and assets. By that measure, platform businesses are paradoxical: 'Uber, the world's largest taxi company, owns no vehicles. Facebook, the world's most popular media owner, creates no content. Alibaba, the most valuable retailer, has no inventory. And Airbnb, the world's largest accommodation provider, owns no real estate.'[7] In place of stock and assets, these are Internet interfaces that connect customers to sole traders and small businesses with stock and assets. To varying degrees the platforms may set certain terms of work such as prices per hour or payment handling or the vetting of providers. On the other hand, those who deliver services through a platform are free in a way that a wage or salary employee is not: they set their own hours of work and can refuse to take on prospective clients or assignments. If they do not enjoy such freedoms then they are liable to be classified under law as an employee rather than an independent contractor.

A mainly post-2008 phenomenon, platform capitalism is mediated by smartphone applications. These allow vendors, customers and the platform third party to interact swiftly and efficiently.[8] As it has evolved, platform capitalism has begun to provide a simple way for individuals to turn personal household assets — such as cars, computers, houses, tools, or even residential power generation devices — into income-generating capital assets. This is sometimes mistakenly described as a 'sharing economy' as if it was a kind of contemporary mutualism or cooperative socialism. It is not. Christopher Koopman described the economic model well when he said that it 'allows people to take idle capital and turn them into revenue sources. People are taking spare bedrooms, cars, tools they are not using and becoming their own entrepreneurs'.[9] This activates otherwise inactive capital. It wakes up dormant capital assets from their slumbers.

Mostly this is small capital and the owners of this capital are typically sole traders. In service industries (like deliveries or cleaning) the returns to the contractors are not great because these industries do not require high skills (proficiency and pleasantness, yes; but this is not the kind of work that delivers high returns per hour). It can be argued that phone-mediated ride-cleaning-and-delivery services are a poor substitute for lost corporate and industrial work.[10] But the long-term trend has been for manufacturing work to be replaced by machines. Automation is now doing the same to office work. Platform capitalism makes it easier for those in low-income occupations to self-organize work. It expands the range of that work by inventing new occupations like the valet delivery person. It also points to a more fundamental social fact: as the service sector is automated, income will increasingly depend on capital (assets) rather than labour.

Capital does not necessarily mean big capital. It means tools and machines. It is less labour and more machines that in the future will generate income. In the transport sector truck drivers will disappear. Owner-drivers will no longer exist but owner-managers will.[11] Truck owning will not just mean possession of property but its oversight, maintenance, tracking, contracting and so on. Or take the taxi industry. Uber today intermediates consumers and the owner-drivers of cars. The Uber of the future will intermediate consumers and the owners of driverless cars. In this social model, income derives from the ownership of capital rather than labour — though owning capital in this case also means doing things. The long-term increase in household capitalisation facilitates this.[12]

As the price of capital over time has come down, it has become easier to own assets. The economics (even the definition) of the new generation of capital work is still to be settled. Parties argue about the median income of Uber 'share' drivers or house owners who rent their property through the AirBnB platform. Is this income simply supplemental in scale (a kind of pocket money) or can it convincingly generate a full-time income? Are these weekend hobby businesses and ersatz moonlighting work? Or is there some deeper shift going on? The persons who perform paid services through platforms — are they independent contractors, employees, or actually some new category of gainfully employed person? What these persons do seems to fit uncomfortably into prevailing legal and vernacular categories. Perhaps those categories are inadequate to fully describe an emerging economy.

The increase in capital work is consistent with the longer-term, larger-scale economic trend that has seen an increase in the income that accrues to capital as opposed to labour. The French economist Thomas Piketty has argued that the rate of return to capital over the long term has grown compared with the return accruing to wages.[13] Piketty supposes that this trend is a negative one. He assumes that the return on capital is bad and the return on labour is good. This is a moral assumption that arguably is wrong. In fact we have reached the point in advanced economies where most people have personal assets that can be turned into income-generating capital in the same sense that everyone more or less has the capacity to labour and to generate income from labour. Not only that but also the rise of micro businesses and sole trading in advanced economies on a large scale points to derivative social benefits. These enterprises significantly overlap with home-based work. Because much of this work is telecom-based and telecommuting in nature, it reduces regular commuting. IT is a facilitator of platform capitalism. IT allows persons to work 'anytime, anywhere'. This capacity has begun to break down the office–home distinction that emerged on a large scale in the late nineteenth century.[14] Telecommuting is an effective work mode just as digital communication is an efficient way of buying and selling goods and services.[15] A 1 percent reduction in road use equates a 3 percent reduction in road congestion. Half-time tele-work would annually save the estimated equivalent of 1,600 lives and prevent 99,000 injuries in the United States and reduce the direct and indirect costs of traffic accidents by $12 billion a year.[16]

The long-term shift from salaried work to capital work is reflected in a rise in the numbers of sole proprietors and legal partnerships. In 1995, 16,423,000 sole proprietor tax returns were lodged with the American IRS. In 2012, the number was 23,426,000, an increase of 42 percent in 18 years. Meanwhile the population of the United States increased by 22 percent only. Over the same interval the total business receipts of sole traders grew from $807 billion to $1,301 billion outpacing inflation by 7 percent.[17] Just as sole proprietorships have grown significantly so have partnerships. Between 2003 and 2012, the US population increased 8 percent while the number of partnerships reporting to the IRS increased 42 percent from 2,375,375 to 3,388,561. Net income of these partnerships over the same period grew 258 percent from $301,398,218,000 in 2003 to $777,924,476,000 in 2012, outpacing inflation by 100 percent.[18] Generally speaking, small business growth is today the key to employment growth. In the United States, 1 percent of companies generate 40 percent of new jobs in any year, and two-thirds of that 1 percent of companies are young. They are less than 5 years old. Many of these are small companies, and many of them will remain small.[19]

Flexible occupations — which include the spectrum of freelance, temporary work, contract work, independent contractors, project-based contractors, entrepreneurs and business owners — are growing globally as is the interest in flexible and non-traditional occupational models.[20] This runs parallel with the appeal of cross-functional (cross-discipline) work, remote working, flexible schedules and working with mobile equipment and technology. A 2009 estimate reckoned that 20 percent of the workforce was self-employed across 29 countries in Europe, North America and the Asia-Pacific.[21] Estimates are difficult as self-employment often overlaps with salaried employment. Somewhere between 35 and 40 percent of the US workforce will engage at some times in self-employment. Eleven percent of US workforce (17.9 million) works 15 hours or more a week in self-employment. Most of this number work more than 35 hours a week.[22] Another 7 percent work less than 15 hours a week in self-employment. In the United Kingdom, the total number of self-employed is 14.7 percent. In the United Kingdom across 2011–14, self-employment grew by 14.2 percent compared with the 4.2 percent growth in wage-and-salary employees.[23] This reflects an increasingly entrepreneurial economy.[24] In the United States, self-employment likewise is growing much faster than the salaried workforce, up 12.5 percent since 2011, compared with 1.1 percent for the total US labour force.[25] Also in the Czech Republic, Estonia, Finland, France and the Netherlands, self-employment grew between 2005 and 2014.[26]

Self-employment in the range of 10–15 percent is not reflected everywhere (yet). In Australia, the number of sole traders rose from 6.7 percent of the workforce in 1978 to 9 percent in 2013. The number of self-employed who employed others declined from 11.8 percent in 1998 to 8.7 percent in 2013.[27] This contradictory trend pointed to a mild shift in Australia's overall occupational profile away from capital work, though the statistical classification of the self-employed at times is murky. Australia's population grew from 17.8 million in 1994 to 20.8 million in 2007, a 16 percent increase. The number of full-time and part-time 'owner-managers' of incorporated and unincorporated enterprises in the period grew by 22 percent from 1,592,000 to 1,951,000, while the number of full-time and part-time wage-and-salary workers grew by 26 percent from 6,661,000 to 8,456,000.[28] Overall, Australia retained a bias towards salaried work while the United States and the United Kingdom were shifting incrementally towards capital work. The pervasiveness of machines in an auto-industrial society will further stimulate the trend towards capital work.

AUTOMATION AND THE LONG STAGNATION

Modern capitalist economies are based on the paradox that 'less is more'. The art of economizing is to produce more goods or services with less labour input. A successful modern economy has high levels of productivity. Each year it produces more goods and services utilizing less labour per unit of production. Using less labour in this manner creates a conundrum. Increases in productivity make a society wealthier. But if 'less labour' means that the net stock of work in a society shrinks then the general level of social prosperity will reduce. The puzzle of modern industrial capitalism is how these economies increase productivity and wealth yet ensure that the benefits of wealth are broadly distributed through work and occupation.

Modern capitalism is an innovation-propelled economic system. It relies on an imaginative impulse. This expresses itself in two ways. Productivity is an elemental form of creativity. To achieve more output with less input requires ingenuity. Thinking up resourceful ways of producing the same quantity of goods and services with fewer employees is a clever form of problem solving. But it is also one dimension only of the larger wellspring of ingenuity that successful capitalist economies rely on. For they have to constantly engage in an act of double coding. While they reduce labour inputs they increase the range and kinds of economic activity. A society can use out-of-work labour in new industries.

Alternatively it can divert labour into capital work. Fewer persons may engage in salaried work or wage work for a living, yet remain usefully occupied if more individuals engage in capital work as sole traders, partnerships, unincorporated and incorporated businesses and the like.

Capital work represents the time that the owner of capital spends managing, coordinating, organizing and directing an investment or business.[29] Modern societies over time alter the relativities between income that is earned respectively by labour and capital. Likewise the demand for wage labour and capital work varies. When the number of people earning income from capital relative to wage labour increases, the effect is what is sometimes called popular capitalism. This reduces the reliance of society on wages or salaries as the means of distributing the benefits of productivity gains. This entails more people earning income as sole traders, in partnerships or as the owners of small and medium-sized businesses.

Creativity is hard. The increase in wealth and productivity in modern capitalist economies has been dramatic over the past two hundred years. It has pulled a large portion of the world's population out of absolute poverty and given the citizens of advanced and many mid-tier economies a standard of living unparalleled in human history.[30] The economic advancement of the past two centuries is remarkable. But it is also difficult to sustain. This is because it requires constant innovation. This is another paradox of modern capitalism. Its enduring bedrock principle is ingenuity. Such ingenuity produces new things. Those new things if they are successful become durable, stable and permanent features of the lives of people. Often such things, when they are first experienced, feel like 'the shock of the new'.[31] But such shock eventually turns to acceptance. What at first is astonishing eventually becomes routine. This double-edged quality of modern capitalism is a key to its success. This 'double edge' is in fact very much like creativity itself. What the act of creation does is to join together what ordinarily is set apart.[32] That is how interesting things are created and added to the world.

A core challenge for modern economies is to be continuously creative. This is more or less impossible in a literal sense. It means that modern capitalism is not progressive but rather cyclical.[33] It does not operate along a straight line of improvement. Instead it goes up and down and up and down. When it goes up, people expect it to keep going up. When it does down, the same people expect it to keep going down. The ideology of progressivism is one of the chief obstacles to understanding the peculiar dynamics of modern industrial capitalist economies. These economies are neither progressive nor regressive. They do not move in one direction only. Rather they move in two directions simultaneously. This is another aspect of the double-coding of modern capitalism.[34] Its cyclical nature is a practical form of economic dual-coding. The downturns of capitalist economies, as stressful as they might be when they are experienced, are essential sources of the upturns that follow them. Upturns are born of downturns, and vice versa. Downturns signal that a generation of innovation has exhausted its potential.

Economic downturns reduce the demand for labour. Jobs that were previously thought of as necessary are dispensed with. Once they go, these jobs rarely return in the same numbers to an economy. Businesses and organizations discover, often painfully, that they can do more with less. They might not go seeking it but the mechanism of economic cycles imposes efficiencies on business units. Due to the pressure of economic circumstances, a business discovers that a new generation of machines can replace the employees that were let go at the bottom of the economic cycle. Modern capitalism is technological in nature. It is a species of industrialism. It saves on the cost of labour by using machines. Machines that replace labour allow economies to produce more with less. That is part of the way in which a dynamic economy works. But capitalism does not only shed labour. It is also inventive in creating new kinds of work in new kinds of industries.

At one time the automobile industry was a new industry; likewise the aircraft industry. At first their need for labour expanded; then as they matured and automated, it reduced. This cycle repeats. The IT industry in the 1980s though hinted at something different. Namely that while new industries might increase labour demand, this might not be on the historical scale of the railways or automobile industry. It is because of this that capitalism's propensity to generate capital work proves to be as crucial as the creation of additional wage-work in fresh industries. Arguably, future employment in the auto-industrial age rests as much on capital work as it does on newfound wage-and-salary work. This supposes that persons switch to earning from capital rather than labour. Income of this kind includes royalties, dividends, interest, capital gains, rents, profits and income derived from household capitalisation.[35] The purchase and maintaining of a second or third home to rent, as a long-term investment, is now a common practice among modest mid-income households, supplementing wage earnings.[36] Capital work of this kind underscores modern capitalism's double-coding. It can reduce the demand for labour and increase the demand for work at the same time.

In 2008 the global economy settled into a long phase of economic stagnation. This was characterized by lower growth, lower productivity, stagnant real incomes, a reduction in economic demand and the shedding of labour. Even in China, the most bullish of the major world economies, growth declined. The period of global stagnation was framed by a longer-run decline in productivity and shrinking rates of economic growth in major economies. This was evident well before the global downturn of 2008.[37] High rates of growth enable countries to increase their GDP per capita. They get richer. With that, social prosperity grows. Lower growth is manifest in the flat-lining of real incomes and in unemployment, underemployment and declines in labour participation rates. One explanation of multi-decade declining productivity is the growth of post-industrial service jobs in advanced economies. These proved difficult to make more productive.[38] A hairdresser today is not much more productive than 50 years ago. The growth of the government, education and health sectors in the post-industrial era was accompanied by a multiplication of regulations and procedures. This also stymied productivity gains.[39]

This scenario may change. While low growth is acutely visible in advanced economies today, less visible is the accelerating replacement of labour by machines.[40] Contemporary labour substitution takes the form of automation, computerization and robotics. This is built on long-existing technologies. Computing and robotics were both well established by the 1950s. In the 2010s, their labour-replacing power accelerated. This kind of long-run development punctuated by a late-arriving sharp upswing is true of many major technology impacts. Rarely are these overnight stories. In fact, automation is as old as industrialism. What is interesting about the post-2008 acceleration of automation is what it focuses on. It targets routine work on a large scale. This includes both repetitive manual work in the case of robotics and repetitive white-collar office work in the case of computerization. Across the medium term of 10–20 years (2008–30) the amount of routine work expected to be replaced is large indeed.[41] Thirty to forty percent of existing jobs will be affected in major ways, suggesting that, in net terms, at least 20 percent of existing work will be completely eliminated.

The process of reducing routine work has been going on beneath the economic surface in advanced economies since 1990.[42] In each succeeding cyclical downturn since then, a portion of the total volume of repetitive work has been replaced by machines. This labour substitution was disguised by the simultaneous growth of government and corporate regulation. Productivity gains through automation were negated by the post-industrial expansion of private and public bureaucracies. Even when government, health and education sectors and corporations got more efficient, they also got less efficient. In the 1980s, socialism as a political idea collapsed. After that, though, regulation flourished. The aggressive expansion of regulation in advanced economies generated routine work functions. Checking, auditing, reviewing, inspecting, assessing, appraising and examining became the primary growth industry of the 1990s and 2000s in major economies. As this happened, though, the technology was developing to eventually automate these functions. Today online processing of routine customer applications by government is one-thirtieth the cost of doing the same operation in-person face-to-face.[43] Offshoring the application process is by comparison only one-fifth the cost of a face-to-face transaction. Consequently, the balance between the multiplication of routine functions and their automation is now shifting decisively in favour of automation.

In economies like the United States automating routine work has produced the phenomenon of 'job polarization'. Jobs at the top-and-bottom ends of the work skill spectrum have grown since 1990; demand for routine mid-tier, mid-skill work, notably in offices, has declined — and is projected to decline further.[44] The result has been a hollowing-out of middle-class jobs with the prospect that many more such occupations will disappear over the next two decades. Since 1990, low-income service work has been less affected by automation. It is often not routine enough to be replaced by the current generation of machines. But with rapid advances in robotics in the last decade (2006–16) that is changing. Increasing swathes of routine work of all kinds, manual and non-manual, are likely to be replaced by machines in the near- and medium-term future. The scale of this replacement is significant.

The execution of routine work involves repetitive and well-defined steps. Such steps can be mimicked by computer algorithms. Once that is achieved the work can be done by machines. Software is progressively replacing mid-tier accounting, HR, payroll, tax agent, travel agent, clerical processing and multiple similar functions. As machine intelligence has improved and sensor technology has grown cheaper and better, advances in autonomous robotic systems are replacing ever-increasing numbers of mobile and manual operations with machines. Autonomous cars, military vehicles and aircraft along with domestic, factory and hospital robot assistants are appearing. In 30 years' time, road and transport systems to a significant extent will be driverless and operatorless. New markets and systems for autonomous car rental in part-place of car ownership will arise.[45] Peopleless systems of factories-warehousing-transport-retail lie not too far into the future. Robots are still poor at carrying out tasks that involve high levels of manual dexterity. With time the dexterity of the machines will also grow.

Machines replacing labour represents one side of the dual-sided system of economic innovation. This is 'disruptive innovation'. It makes the production, distribution and allocation of things more efficient and commodious by doing more with less. Advanced economies today are accelerating the pace at which they are replacing routine labour with machines. These economies are moving from the post-industrial to the auto-industrial era. The post-industrial era was characterized by the expansion of 'knowledge work'. This was university-qualified mid-tier, mid-skill, information-processing, office-based work. The expansion of such work is over. It is now contracting. Machines are replacing office workers. In London between 2001 and 2013, 65 percent of library assistants, 48 percent of counter clerks and 44 percent of PAs disappeared.[46]

This is one side of modern economic dynamism. Technology innovation 'disrupts' by enabling existing functions to be done more cheaply, more quickly and more simply by machines. The other side of the capitalist economic cycle is 'constructive innovation'. As some areas of an economy shrink, others grow. Economies in the foreseeable near term are likely to see expansion occur in the calculation, care and construction industries. These sectors are not immune from automation, far from it. But employment in these fields is expanding faster than technology is shrinking them. In the longer term, the DIY autonomous economy shows promise of taking up the slack left by a shrinking tertiary service and office economy. The quaternary economy is the most powerful substitute in the long term as the previously labour-intensive tertiary economy replaces office labour with machines.

Capital work is a key to future constructive innovation. As machines become ever more pervasive, occupations will focus more on the ownership of capital and its attendant roles, those of maintaining and coordinating the use of the capital.[47] The alternative to newfound salaried work is forms of capital work. Income accruing to capital (via dividends, rents, profits, interest, royalties, owners' draw, partner share, etc.) as a portion of total national income in the major economies in the eighteenth and nineteenth centuries was significant and steady over time. Income generated by capital then declined sharply in the twentieth century (from 1910 onwards). It grew again after 1970.[48] That capital work shrank in the first part of the twentieth century is not surprising. The nineteenth century was the era of liberal capitalism. The first half of the twentieth century was the age of socialism. Socialism despised income from capital while it eulogized income from wage labour. The share of national income in major economies echoed this political disposition. Then something happened in 1970. After that date, the portion of income from capital grew again.

This in part reflected the decline of socialism, though it also reflected the way in which socialism's agenda was replaced by regulation in the post-industrial era. The post-industrial era saw the proliferation of regulatory and process bureaucracies. This was the kind of salaried work that delivered few productivity gains. Accordingly the income it generated over time stagnated. The tacit response of many individuals to this was to move away from salaried work. There is every indication that, in the age of auto-industrialism, capital's share of income will rise.

Emerging alongside auto-industrialism is the autonomous economy. One responds to the other. Self-starting, DIY, self-employing businesses, including high-tech cottage industries and garage enterprises, are expanding. There are distinct signs that the age of the office is coming to an end. White-collar work and pink-collar work are being automated. Big businesses and large organizations increasingly rely on machines rather than personnel to carry out routine processing. This will increase over time. As it does, work that is not automated or that cannot be automated will gravitate to small, medium and household enterprises. This implies a big cultural shift. This shift will not happen readily. Post-industrial ideology is deeply embedded in peak modern societies. The post-modern, post-industrial world is one of procedures, process and regulation. It is bureaucratic in nature. Initiative, self-organization and autonomy play almost no part in it. This runs up against the logic of the quaternary economy.

From the standpoint of small and medium business and the self-employed, post-industrial administrative offices and systems represent costs not benefits. Words like 'health' and 'education' conjure up beneficial images of 'being healed' and 'learning things'. Yet what they have come to involve in practice are expensive and elaborate processes and procedures. Auto-industrialism presents a fundamental challenge to this. It automates processes. It removes the need for a large office-and-administrative class. It opens up the possibility of significantly reducing the size of the administrative state and at the same time expanding the size of the quaternary autonomous economy. In so doing, it promises to reduce bureaucratic self-abnegation and increase the quantum of human happiness.

NOTES

1. Kotkin (2014: chapter 7).
2. Pickman and Viek (2014).
3. From 12 percent in 1969 to 26 percent in 2009.
4. For historical levels of US self-employment, see Hipple (2004).

5. Blair (1946: 14). See also Applebaum (1998: 134).
6. The heart of a self-organizing association is not rules but patterns. Rules are a function of governance. Patterns are an attribute of nature and art. Rules can be replicated by software algorithms. These structure repeating automated tasks. Patterns in contrast are the stuff of creation. What cannot be automated is pattern creation. This is the art that lies at the heart of human work and action.
7. Goodwin (2015).
8. Uber was founded in 2009; AirBnB in 2008; Taskrabbit in 2008; Homejoy in 2010; Instacart in 2012; Postmates in 2011.
9. AFP report in the *Daily Mail Australia*, 4 February 2015.
10. Asher-Schapiro (2015).
11. Freeman (2015) observes: 'Workers can benefit from technology that substitutes robots or other machines for their work by owning part of the capital that replaces them … As companies substitute machines and computers for human activity, workers need to own part of the capital stock that substitutes for them to benefit from these new "robot" technologies.'
12. The American sociologist Talcott Parsons noted as early as 1961 (1964: 230) the phenomenon of household capitalisation that underlies self-employment aggregators like Uber that allow persons to switch household consumption items, like the automobile, into productive capital.
13. Piketty (2014). Benzell, Kotlikoff, LaGarda and Sachs (2015) similarly conclude that 'a long-run decline in labor share of income' appears to be underway among OECD members.
14. Office work clearly separated from households effectively begins with the East India Company in the late eighteenth century, but it is another century before we see the construction of purpose-specific office buildings on a large scale.
15. For the pros and cons of telecommuting, see the summation of 500 studies on the subject outlined by Global Workplace Analytics, Costs and Benefits: advantages of telecommuting for companies.
16. Global Workplace Analytics, Costs and Benefits: advantages of telecommuting for companies.
17. Internal Revenue Service sole proprietorship returns 1996 and 2012.
18. Internal Revenue Service partnership returns 2003 and 2012.
19. Stangler (2010: 5–7).
20. Kelly (2014). The Kelly report draws on an annual global workforce survey of over 200,000 respondents in more than 30 countries.
21. Kelly (2009).
22. Johnson (2013); MBO Partners (2014).
23. Committee for Economic Development of Australia (2015: 184).
24. The United Kingdom had one company for every 70 persons in 1979; in 2016 the figure was one company for every 17 persons. The United Kingdom today has 10 percent of the population of Europe, but 40 percent of its 'unicorns', start-ups valued at $1 billion or more. Lynn (2016).

25. MBO Partners (2014: 6).
26. World Bank, self-employed, total (percentage of total employed).
27. Committee for Economic Development of Australia (2015: 180).
28. Australian Bureau of Statistics employment type: employed persons by sex, full-time/part-time and industry (ANZSIC 1993), August 1994 to August 2007, table 5.
29. Today the largest cohorts of sole proprietors in the United States are in descending order of size: professional scientific and technical services 13 percent; services 12 percent; construction 11 percent; administration 10 percent; retail 9 percent; health 9 percent; arts, entertainment and recreation 6 percent. Source: Internal Revenue Service sole proprietorship returns, 2012.
30. McCloskey (2010: 86–90).
31. The term was immortalized by Robert Hughes (1991).
32. Murphy (2012: 82–96).
33. Murphy (2012: 149–92).
34. Murphy (2014a: 71–89).
35. Arguably it also includes operator salaries, which are defined as business expenditure for tax purposes but are also key items of income for many sole proprietors and partners.
36. In 2011, 15 percent or 1.7 million Australians out of a working population of 11 million owned an investment property; in the United Kingdom in 2010–11, 6 percent (1.9 million persons out of a working population of 31.75 million) paid tax on rental income; in the United States in 2005, 6 percent or 9.1 million taxpayers reported rental income to the IRS out of an adult working population of 150 million. Data sources: ATO; UK HMRC; US General Accounting Office.
37. Piketty (2014: 93–6).
38. '…productivity growth in the service sector has generally been low (or even zero in some cases, which explains why this sector has tended to employ a steadily increasing share of the workforce)'. Piketty (2014: 90).
39. Murphy (2015a).
40. Autor and Dorn (2013: 1553–97); Deloitte (2014); Sui and Jaimovich (2015).
41. Frey and Osborne (2013, 2015); Committee for Economic Development of Australia (2015).
42. Sui and Jaimovich (2015); Autor, Levy and Murnane (2003); Autor, Katz and Kearney (2006).
43. Deloitte Access Economics (2015, table 3.1).
44. Frey and Osborne (2013, 2015); Committee for Economic Development of Australia (2015); Autor and Dorn (2013); Deloitte (2014); Sui and Jaimovich (2015).
45. The advantage of short-term car rental over long-term car ownership is that private cars are idle 96 percent of the time (Kelman, 2016). An app-based ordering system that guaranteed on-time arrival of driverless vehicles makes short-term car renting a viable proposition on a mass scale. McKinsey (2016) notes that already there are 'significant, early signs that the importance of private car ownership is declining and shared mobility is increasing … in the US the share of young people (16 to 24 years)

that hold a driver's license dropped from 76 percent in 2000 to 71 percent in 2013, while the number of car sharing members in North America and Germany has grown by more than 30 percent annually over the last five years.' McKinsey calculates that 'up to one out of ten new cars sold in 2030 may likely be a shared vehicle, which could reduce private use vehicle sales, an effect partially offset by a faster replacement rate for shared vehicles. This would mean that more than 30 percent of miles driven in new cars sold could be from shared mobility. On this trajectory, one out of three new cars sold could potentially be a shared vehicle as soon as 2050'.

46. Deloitte (2014, figure 4).
47. Rotman (2015) puts it aptly: 'Whoever owns the capital will benefit as robots and AI inevitably replace many jobs.'
48. Piketty (2014, figure 3.5).

REFERENCES

Acemoglu, D. and Autor, D. (2012) 'What does human capital do?', *Journal of Economic Literature*, 50 (2): 426–63.

Administrative Review Council. (2014) *Automated Assistance in Administrative Decision Making*. Canberra: Australian Government.

Anderson, C. (2012) *Makers: The New Industrial Revolution*. New York: Random House Business Books.

Applebaum, H.A. (1998) *The American Work Ethic and the Changing Work Force*. Westport, CT: Greenwood.

AppraisalEconomics. (2015) *Social Media Valuation and the Value of a User*. Paramus, NJ: AppraisalEconomics.

Asher-Schapiro, A. (2015) 'The sharing economy is propaganda', *Cato Unbound: A Journal of Debate*, 13 February.

Ashton, A.H., Ashton, R.H. and Davis, M.N. (1994) 'White-collar robotics', *California Management Review*, 37 (1): 83–109.

Australian Institute of Health and Welfare (AIHW). (2016) *25 Years of Health Expenditure in Australia 1989–90 to 2013–14*. Canberra: AIHW.

Automated Assistance in Administrative Decision-Making Working Group. (2007) *Automated Assistance in Administrative Decision-Making*. Canberra: Australian Government.

Autor, D. and Dorn, D. (2013) 'The growth of low-skill service jobs and the polarization of the U.S. labor market', *American Economic Review*, 103 (5): 1553–97.

Autor, D.H. (2014) 'Skills, education, and the rise of earnings inequality among the "other 99 percent"', *Science*, 344 (6186): 843–51.

Autor, D.H., Katz, L.F. and Kearney, M.S. (2006) 'The polarization of the U.S. labor market', *American Economic Review Papers and Proceedings*, 96 (2): 189–94.

Autor, D.H., Levy, F. and Murnane, R.L. (2003) 'The skill content of recent technological change: an empirical exploration', *Quarterly Journal of Economics*, 118 (4): 1279–333.

Baily, N.M. and Bosworth, B.P. (2014) 'US manufacturing: understanding its past and its potential future', *Journal of Economic Perspectives*, 28 (1): 3–26.

Barea, D. and Vasudeva, P. (2015) *Will Today's Graduates Want to Work for You?* London: Accenture.

Bennett, J. and Lotus, M. (2013) *America 3.0: Rebooting American Prosperity in the 21st Century*. New York: Encounter Books.

Benzell, S.G., Kotlikoff, L.J., LaGarda, G. and Sachs, J.D. (2015) *Robots Are Us: Some Economics of Human Replacement NBER Working Paper No. 20941*. Cambridge: National Bureau of Economic Research.

Betbeze, P. (2012) 'Automation and the Healthcare Cost Curve', *Health Leaders Media*, 30 April.

Blair, J. (1946) *Economic Concentration and World War II*. Washington, DC: US Senate.

Boccia, R. (2015) '1 in 20 of working-age Americans receives disability benefits', *The Daily Signal*, 11 April.

Bodkin, H. (2016) '"Origami robot" can be swallowed in pill and then sent on missions in the human body', *The Telegraph*, 13 May.

Borghina, D. (2015) 'Volvo's robots will quietly pick up and empty your garbage bin', *Gizmag*, 21 September.

Bowker. (2014) *Self-Publishing in the United States*. New Providence, NJ: Bowker.

Brown, R. (1984) *The Nature of Social Laws: From Machiavelli to J.S. Mill*. Cambridge: Cambridge University Press.

Brynjolfsson, E. and McAfee, A. (2014) *The Second Machine Age*. New York: W. W. Norton.

Burnham, J. (1941) *The Managerial Revolution*. New York: John Day.

Burnham, J. (1943) *The Machiavellians*. New York: John Day.

Burnham, J. (2014[1964]) *Suicide of the West*. New York: Encounter Books.

Cavendish, L. (2015) 'My son doesn't want to go to university', *The Telegraph*, 14 July.

Centre for Retail Research (CRR). (2015) *Online Retailing: Britain, Europe, US and Canada 2015*. Newark: CRR.

Chan, S.P. (2016) 'Robots are coming for your job', *The Telegraph*, 21 January.

Chapman, M. (2014) 'Radical change ahead for tax agents', *Taxpayers Australia Limited*, 7 July.

Chatham, C. (2007) '10 important differences between brains and computers', *Developing Intelligence* blog, 27 March.

Chobanov, D. and Mladenova, A. (2009) *What is the Optimum Size of Government*. Bulgaria: Institute for Market Economics.

Committee for Economic Development of Australia (CEDA). (2015) *Australia's Future Workforce?* Melbourne: CEDA.

Congressional Budget Office (2016) *The Distribution of Household Income and Federal Taxes, 2013*, 8 June.

Cost, J. (2015) 'What the hell is going on? The fraying of the national political consensus', *The Weekly Standard*, 12 October.

Cowen, T. (2013) *Average Is Over: Powering America Beyond the Age of the Great Stagnation*. New York: Penguin.

Crawford, B. (2014) 'Design: I, robot, will mow your lawn', *New Zealand Herald*, 29 June.

Creighton, A. (2016) 'Bureaucrats weigh on health as number of administrators blows out', *The Australian*, 29 April.

Cribb, J., Disney, R. and Sibieta, L. (2014) *The Public Sector Workforce: Past, Present and Future IFS Briefing Note BN145*. London: Institute for Fiscal Studies.

Cunliffe, R. (2015) 'Is there anything Estonians can't do online?', *CapX*, 2 July.

Dabla-Norris, E., Kochhar, K., Ricka, F., Suphaphiphat, N. and Tsounta, E. (2015) *Causes and Consequences of Inequality*. Washington, DC: IMF.

Davidson, K. (2015) 'Generation Y or generation DIY', *Frock Paper Scissors*.

Deloitte. (2014) *London Futures*. London: Deloitte.

Deloitte. (2015a) *From Brawn to Brains: The Impact of Technology on Jobs in the UK*. London: Deloitte LLP.

Deloitte. (2015b) *Technology and People: The Great Job-Creating Machine*. London: Deloitte LLP.

Deloitte Access Economics. (2014) *Building the Lucky Country #3: Positioning for Prosperity*. Sydney: Deloitte.

Deloitte Access Economics. (2015) *Digital Government Transformation*. Sydney: Deloitte.

Demetriou, D. (2015) 'Robot hotel', *The Telegraph*, 16 July.

Dennis, M.J. (2014) 'Competency-based degrees', *University World News*, 307.

Dewey, J. (1948[1920]) *Reconstruction in Philosophy*. Boston: Beacon Press.

Dewey, J. (1959[1929]) *Experience and Nature*. New York: Dover.

Di Matteo, L. (2013) *Measuring Government in the Twenty-first Century*. Toronto, The Fraser Institute.

Dujmovic, J. (2016) 'This tiny country is the most technologically advanced in the world', *Market Watch*, 9 July.

Dyer, J., Gregersen, H. and Christensen, C.M. (2011) *The Innovator's DNA: Mastering the Five Skills of Disruptive Innovators*. Boston, MA: Harvard Business Review Press.

Epistemic Games. (2013) 'School ATMs: automated teaching machines?', *GAPS: Games and Professional Simulations Research Consortium*. http://edgaps.org/gaps/

Farage, N. (2015) 'Nigel Farage: we bought when we meant to sell and lost millions', *The Telegraph*, 14 March.

Ford, M. (2015) *The Rise of the Robots*. London: OneWorld.

Freeman, R.B. (2015) 'Who owns the robots rules the world', *IZA World of Labor*, 5.

Frey, C.B. and Osborne, M.A. (2013) *The Future of Employment*. Oxford: Oxford Martin School.

Frey, C.B. and Osborne, M.A. (2015) *Technology at Work*. Oxford: Oxford Martin School.

Freyberg, T. (2011) 'Rise of the machines', *Waste Management World*, 11 October.

Friedman, T.L. and Mandelbaum, M. (2011) *That Used To Be Us*. London: Little, Brown.

Fromm, J. (2013) 'Generation Y has become generation DIY', *Millennial Marketing* blog.

Fry, S. (2015) 'When Stephen Fry met Jony Ive', *The Telegraph*, 25 May.

Gandhi, R. (2015) 'Avoid these 7 mistakes when pitching to big-time VCs', *Entrepreneur*, 24 November.

Gates, B. (2007) 'A robot in every home', *Scientific American*, January: 58–65.

Gerhardt, W. (2008) *Prosumers: A New Growth Opportunity*. San Jose, CA: Cisco Systems Internet Business Solutions Group.

Gilmore, H. and Knott, M. (2014) 'Business head calls for fewer uni students', *Sydney Morning Herald*, 4 August.

Glover, J. (2011) 'Investigating "hybrid" jobs in IT: A "Third Way" skills set?', *Bcs. Org*, January.

Goodwin, T. (2015) 'The battle is for the customer interface', *Crunch Network* blog, 3 March.

Goos, M. and Manning, A. (2003) *Lousy and Lovely Jobs: The Rising Polarization of Work in Britain. Discussion Paper No. DP0604.* London: LSE Centre for Economic Performance.

Gordon, R. (2016) 'Will America's slow-growth economy ever get better? Interview with James Pethakoukis', *Ricochet Political Economy Podcast*, 26 January.

Graetz, G. and Michaels, G. (2015) *Robots at Work CEP Discussion Paper No 1335.* London: LSE.

Grose, J. (2013) 'Please, pinterest, stop telling me how to repurpose Mason Jars: DIY culture, homemaking, and the end of expertise', *New Republic*, 5 August.

Guest Writer. (2014) 'ATO warns of radical change ahead for tax agents', *Digital First*, 11 July.

Haksever, C. and Render, B. (2013) *Service Management: An Integrated Approach to Supply Chain Management and Operations.* Upper Saddle River, NJ: Pearson.

Hicks, J. (2013) 'Are we ready for a robotic phlebotomist?', *Forbes*, 30 July.

Hilton, S. (2016) *More Human: Designing a World Where People Come First.* London: WH Allen.

Hipple, S. (2004) 'Self-employment in the United States: an update', *Monthly Labor Review*, July.

Hofstadter, D. and Sander, E. (2013) *Surfaces and Essences: Analogy as the Fuel and Fire of Thinking.* London: Basic Books.

Hughes, R. (1991) *The Shock of the New. Enlarged Edition.* London: Thames and Hudson.

Ibis. (2015) 'Independent label music production in the US: market research report', *IbisWorld*, August.

Ibis. (2015) 'Nursery and garden stores in the US', *IbisWorld*, December.

Ibis. (2016) 'Consumer electronics stores market research report', *IbisWorld*, January.

Inserra, D. and Rosenzweig, P. (2014) *Continuing Federal Cyber Breaches Warn Against Cybersecurity Regulation Issue Brief #4288 on National Security and Defense.* Washington, DC: Heritage Foundation.

Joe, S. (2013) 'Macy's blueprint for omnichannel dominance', *Retail Info Systems News*, 5 March.

Johnston, P. (2015) 'Iain Duncan Smith, the unlikely champion for workers', *The Telegraph*, 11 July.

Johnson, W. (2013) 'Independent work may be inevitable', *Harvard Business Review*, 19 February.

Jones, P. (2015) 'How big is self-publishing', *The Bookseller*, 16 June.

Hennessey, M. (2016) 'Homeschool for freedom', *National Review*, 14 May.

Kamenetz, A. (2010) *DIY U.* White River Junction, VT: Chelsea Green.

Kassamali, R.H. and Ladak, B. (2015) 'The role of robotics in interventional radiology', *Quantitative Imaging in Medicine and Surgery* 5 (3): 340–3.

Kelly. (2009) *2009 Kelly Global Workforce Index.*

Kelly. (2014) *2014 Kelly Global Workforce Index.*

Kelman, G. (2016) 'The American city was built for cars. What will happen when they all leave?', *LinkedIn*, 30 March.

Kenny, C. (2014) 'Why factory jobs are shrinking everywhere', *Bloomberg*, 28 April.

Kern, F. (2010) 'What Chief Executives Really Want', *Bloomberg Businessweek*, 19 May.

Kohler, M. and van der Merwe, M. (2015) 'Long-run trends in housing price growth', *RBA Bulletin*, September Quarter. Sydney: Reserve Bank of Australia.

Kotkin, J. (2014) *The New Class Conflict*. Candor, NY: Telos Press Publishing.

Leonard, K. (2012) '$30 billion dollar craft industry enjoys resurgence', *TribLive*, 17 November.

Levy, S. (2012) 'Can an algorithm write a better news story than a human reporter?', *Wired*, 24 April.

Lynn, M. (2016) 'Post-Brexit Britain will offer more for start-ups', *The Telegraph*, 11 July.

Mangu-Ward, K. and Manning, A. (2013) 'Can computers replace teachers?', *Reason.com*, 6 April.

MBO Partners. (2014) *2014 State of Independence in America*. Virginia: MBO Partners.

McCardle, M. (2013) 'Four reasons a guaranteed income won't work', *Bloomberg View*, 4 December.

McCarthy, J. (2015) 'Little change in percentage of Americans who own stocks', *Gallup*, 22 April.

McCloskey, D.N. (2010) *Bourgeois Dignity*. Chicago: University of Chicago Press.

McFarland, M. (2016) 'Professor reveals to students that his assistant was an AI all along', *The Sydney Morning Herald*, 13 May.

McKinsey. (2016) *Automotive Revolution: Perspective towards 2030*. New York: McKinsey & Co.

Mitchell, S. (2015) 'Cotton on: the inside story of the retailer's rise to $1.5b in revenue', *Sydney Morning Herald*, 2 April.

Mohdin, A. (2015) 'This robot is going to 3D-print a steel bridge', *IFL Science*, 16 June.

Moura, M.C.P., Smith, S.J. and Belzer, D.B. (2015) '120 years of U.S. residential housing stock and floor space', *PLoS One*, 10 (8): e0134135.

Murphy, P. (2016) 'The Platform University: the destruction and resurrection of universities in the auto-industrial age', in R. Barnett and M. Peters (eds.), *The Global University: A University Reader*. New York: Peter Lang.

Murphy, P. (2001) *Civic Justice: From Ancient Greece to the Modern World*. Amherst, NY: Humanity Books.

Murphy, P. and Roberts, D. (2004) *The Dialectic of Romanticism: A Critique of Modernism*. London: Continuum.

Murphy, P. (2012) *The Collective Imagination: The Creative Spirit of Free Societies*. Farnham: Ashgate.

Murphy, P. (2014a) 'The enigma of capitalism and the French cul-de-sac', *Thesis Eleven: Critical Theory and Historical Sociology*, 124: 71–89.

Murphy, P. (2014b) 'Beautiful minds and ugly buildings: object creation, digital production, and the research university: reflections on the aesthetic ecology of the mind', in M. Peters, T. Besley and D. Araya (eds.), *The New Development Paradigm: Education, Knowledge Economy, and Digital Futures*. New York: Peter Lang. pp. 161–76.

Murphy, P. (2015a) *Universities and Innovation Economies*. Farnham: Ashgate.

Murphy, P. (2015b) 'The stranger society: the case of economic and social development in the tropics', *Budhi: A Journal of Culture and Ideas*, 19: 1–2.

Murphy, P. (2015c) 'Discovery and delivery: time schemas and the Bureaucratic University', in R. Barnett, C. Guzmán-Valenzuela, O.H. Ylijok and P. Gibbs (eds.), *Time and Temporality in the University*. London: Routledge. pp. 137–53.

Nelson, P. (2013) 'The rise of the consumer electronics prosumer', *TechNewsWorld*, 11 February.

Nelson, R. (2007) 'IT project management: infamous failures, classic mistakes, and best practices', *MIS Quarterly Executive*, 6 (2): 67–78.

Newcomer, E. (2015) 'Uber raises funding at $62.5 billion valuation', *Bloomberg Business*, 4 December.

Newell, J. (2016) 'The "who's sure?" state', *Slate*, 2 May.

NoAgenda Homeschool. (2012) 'Why companies should chase the homeschool market', *NoAgenda Homeschool* blog, 28 August.

OECD. (2011) 'Chart B2.1 expenditure on educational institutions as a percentage of GDP for all levels of education (2000 and 2008)', *Education at a Glance*. Paris: OECD.

OECD. (2014) 'How does the United States compare?', *OECD Health Statistics*. Paris: OECD.

Oh, E. (2016) 'New construction robot lays bricks 3 times as fast as human workers', *Arch Daily*, 7 January.

Parsons, T. (1964) 'The Link between Character and Society' [1961]. *Social Structure and Personality*. New York: Free Press.

Peden, E. (1991) 'Productivity in the United States and its relationship to government activity: an analysis of 57 years, 1929–1986', *Public Choice*, 69: 153–73.

Perry, M. (2012) 'Manufacturing's declining share of GDP is a global phenomenon, and it's something to celebrate', *US Chamber of Commerce Foundation* blog, 22 March.

Perry, M. (2013) 'When it comes to home appliances, the "good old days" are now', *AEIdeas,*18 November.

Pethokoukis, J. (2016) 'It's official: a lost decade for the US economy', *AEIdeas*, 29 January.

Pickman, H. and Viek, C. (2014) 'Do-it-yourself economic growth', *Economic Development Journal*, 13 (1): 19–26.

Piketty, T. (2014) *Capital in the Twenty-First Century*. Cambridge: Harvard University Press.

Porter, C. (2013) 'College degree, no class time required', *Wall Street Journal*, 4 January.

Postrel, V. (2003) 'The aesthetic imperative: why the creative shall inherit the economy', *Wired*, 11: 7.

PricewaterhouseCoopers. (2001) *Patients or Paperwork? The Regulatory Burden Facing America's Hospitals*. Chicago: American Hospital Association.

Quantcast. (2014) 'Instagram is where to find democrats online, but don't expect them to vote', *Quantcast* blog, 15 September.

Reuters. (2016) 'US military christens self-driving Sea Hunter warship', *The Guardian*, 8 April.

Reynolds, G. (2014) *The Education Apocalypse: How It Happened and How to Survive It*. New York: Encounter Books.

Rotman, D. (2015) 'Who will own the robots?', *MIT Technology Review*, 16 June.

Sachs, J. (2015) 'How to live happily with robots', *The American Prospect*, Summer.

Sachs, J.D., Benzell, S.G. and LaGarda, G. (2015) *Robots Curse or Blessing? NBER Working Paper No. 21091*. Cambridge: National Bureau of Economic Research.

Saitto, S. (2015) 'Airbnb said to be raising funding at $20 billion valuation', *Bloomberg Technology*, 1 March.

Schmitt, J., Shierholz, H. and Mishel, L. (2013) *Don't Blame the Robots EPI–CEPR Working Paper*. Washington, DC: Economic Policy Institute.

Schwab, K. (2016) *The Fourth Industrial Revolution*. Geneva: World Economic Forum.

Scully, G. (1994) *What is the Optimal Size of Government in the US. NCPA Policy Report No. 188*. Dallas: National Center for Policy Analysis.

ShareSoc. (2016) 'UK stock market statistics', *ShareSoc.Org*

Skorupa, J. (2013) 'Macy's blueprint for omnichannel dominance', *Retail Info Systems News*, 5 March.

Smashing Robotics. (2016) 'Overview of robotic exoskeleton suits for limb movement assist', *SmashingRobotics.com*, 3 February.

Somers, J. (2013) 'The man who would teach machines to think', *Atlantic Quarterly*, November.

Sorrell, M. (2015) 'What Australia can learn about e-government from Estonia', *The Conversation*, 6 October.

Stangler, D. (2010) *High-Growth Firms and the Future of the American Economy*. Kansas City: Kaufman Foundation for Entrepreneurship.

Stewart, I., Debapratim, D. and Cole, A. (2015) *Technology and People: The Great Job-Creating Machine*. London: Deloitte LLP.

Sui, H. and Jaimovich, N. (2015) *Jobless Recoveries*. Washington, DC: Third Way.

Summers, L. (2010) 'Economic progress and economic policy', *Remarks at the Economic Progress Institute*, 13 December.

Taneja, H. (2015) 'Why startups are more successful than ever at unbundling incumbents', *Harvard Business Review*, 18 June.

Tanzi, V. (2005) 'The economic role of the state in the 21st century', *Cato Journal*, 25: 3.

Telegraph Reporters. (2016) 'Delivery droids coming to London pavements as soon as next month', *The Telegraph*, 26 April.

Toffler, A. (1970) *Future Shock*. New York: Random House.

Toffler, A. (1980) *The Third Wave*. New York: Bantam.

Tomaszewski, S. (2015) 'The US navy is about to build new robot submarines', *Vice News*, 17 April.

Vedder, R. and Gallaway, L. (1998) *Government Size and Economic Growth*. Washington, DC: Joint Economic Committee.

Walters, R. (2014) *Cyber Attacks on U.S. Companies in 2014, Issue Brief #4289 on National Security and Defense*. Washington, DC: Heritage Foundation.

Watson, R. (2016) *Digital Versus Human*. London: Scribe.

Wiltz, C. (2013) 'GE to create robotic hospital system to assist with sterilization', *Device Talk* blog, 5 February.

Yoon, E. (2013) 'To spur growth, target profitable "prosumers"', *Harvard Business Review*, 3 January.

Zheng, C. (2015) 'Robots go it alone at factory with no assembly workers', *China Daily USA*, 5 May.

Zhou, C. (2015) 'World-first robot brickie "Hadrian" can build a house in two days', *Real Estate News*, 13 July.

INDEX